SLEEPWALK

Eastern Washington University Press
Spokane and Cheney, Washington

CHRISTOPHER BUCKLEY

Sleepwalk

CALIFORNIA DREAMIN' AND A LAST DANCE WITH THE '60S

Cover and interior design by A.E. Grey
Cover photograph by Paul Schutzer/Getty Images

Library of Congress Cataloging-in-Publication Data

Buckley, Christopher
Sleepwalk : California dreamin' and a last dance with the '60s /
Christopher Buckley.
  p. cm.
ISBN 1-59766-012-4
1. Buckley, Christopher, 1948– —Childhood and youth.
2. Buckley, Christopher, 1948– —Homes and haunts—
California, Southern. 3. Authors, American—20th century—
Biography. 4. Nineteen sixties. 5. United States—Social life
and customs—1945–1970. 6. California, Southern—Intellectual life—20th century. 7. California, Southern—Biography.   I. Title.
PS3552.U339Z46 2006
813'.54—dc22

2006007962

ISBN 1-59766-012-4
Eastern Washington University Press
Spokane and Cheney, Washington

CONTENTS

A child is asleep. Her private life unwinds inside her skin and skull; only as she sheds childhood, first one decade and then another, can she locate the actual, historical stream, see the setting of her dreaming private life—the nation, the city, the neighbor-hood, the house where the family lives—as an actual project under way, a project living people willed, and made well or failed, and are still making, herself among them.

—ANNIE DILLARD, *AN AMERICAN CHILDHOOD*

SLEEP

I was sitting with my mother in the State Theater, in the dark of 1953. Dorothy was clicking the heels of her glittering red shoes, and with her eyes closed kept repeating, prayerlike, "There's no place like home. There's no place like home."

The Wizard of Oz was the first movie I remember seeing, although soon I'd be going to the movies often with my mother and her friends. Those movies were usually for adults, and often I'd doze off in the big theater seats. Five or six is a drowsy age, as you are uncertain of so many things in the world, but I clearly remember telling my mother I wouldn't go with her to *Giant*—James Dean, Elizabeth Taylor, et al.; I was afraid to watch a movie with a menacing GIANT. But of course I went. With my father always gone back to work at night, there was no one to take care of me, and I saw most of the film I think.

Before long, I'd know the State Theater—with its ice-cream stripes of pink, green, and white neon—from the Granada just across the street, with its red, green, and gold marquee fluted high up the building façade. My favorite, the Fox Arlington, was all the way up State Street, with its spires and Spanish arcade, its appliqué of stars winking softly in the night sky above the seats.

But then, I was just five, barely awake in my life, and Dorothy's maxim was mostly lost on me. Kansas looked pretty flat and boring in the dim, black-and-white tornado air, especially when compared to Santa Barbara. Nevertheless, I was relieved when Dorothy woke up to her aunts and uncles and had found her dizzy way back to the farm. Given all that could command a child's attention in that movie—

1

flying monkeys, talking apple trees, Munchkins, the angelic good witch—it was of course the image of the wicked witch that etched itself in my grey matter the most and followed me home. Earlier, in Kansas, on a dour black-and-white road, she was speeding along furiously on a bicycle—all dark whirl and bluster like a storm coming on—having kidnapped Dorothy's little dog. And for more than an hour in living color, she had been trying to prevent Dorothy from reaching Oz, from ever finding her way back home. I was truly relieved when Dorothy gave her the slip, then the hot water melting treatment. It was all moderately terrifying, but finally Dorothy was back in the land she knew, with her relatives, pigtails, gingham dress, dog, and Mary Janes.

We had been living in Santa Barbara for a year and a half, and most of what I could remember was there. I was attending kindergarten at Marymount School on the riviera, the hill in back of town with red-tiled Mediterranean homes dotted among the high eucalyptus stands. I'd badgered my parents to let me go to school ever since I had turned four, and though I was below the minimum age, my parents found this private Catholic school that would admit me. But once in class there were problems—the naps, and the nuns.

Boys were only taken there from kindergarten through second grade, and I remember nuns with pinched cheeks and perpetually sour expressions, and one with a hooked nose who allowed the older girls to steal our hats and sweaters and generally torment us—who told me to be quiet or my parents wouldn't come to pick me up after school and I wouldn't be able to go home. What perverse pleasure must have been theirs, tormenting such easily astonished souls as we. To be fair, some nuns were painless, and there was one very nice one, Madame Adrienne (a French order), who would look after me a bit and take time to toss a ball around as I remained each day after school until 5:30, when my parents could collect me after work. Of course I wasn't then aware of the obvious good/bad witch parallel carrying over from *The Wizard of Oz*. I wasn't aware of very much.

Despite suffering the mean spirits of the hook-nosed nun all day long, the real problem became the nap that kindergarten students were required to take each day after lunch—that brought on true anxiety. I was convinced that if I went to sleep there, I might never see my parents again; there would be no one waiting for me on the other side of the dark when I awoke. It was some insecurity I arrived on the planet with, heavy then on my back as a house. Each night, the light in my room had to be left on in order for me to go to sleep. None of this is all that unusual; I was perhaps just too young to be away from home all day at four and a half or five years old. The one thing I remember my father said to me more than any other was that I had a "big imagination!"

Week to week, I made enough trouble about the nap that my father would sometimes arrive to pick me up from school at 3:00 instead of waiting for my mother to get off from her job at 5:00. He was a DJ, and I expect his hours on the air varied so that he could occasionally slip away from the station. Some days then, he would pull up in our shell-white Pontiac station wagon outside the tall gates to the courtyard for the lower grades; I'd jump into the wide, green vinyl front seat, and we'd head down the winding road. The first thing I would do was unlace my brown school shoes and pull on my black cowboy boots, which I'd left in the car that morning. I did know about cowboys—this was the '50s, and every Saturday morning any household with a TV had good guys and bad guys appropriately dressed and firing six-shooters through a cloud of dust across the black-and-white hills of the Old West, which were located somewhere generally between Chatsworth and Malibu. *Gun Smoke* and *The Cisco Kid* were on once a week, and my boots were like Hopalong Cassidy's, all black with white lilies and red and gilt near the tops. Once I'd pulled them on, I felt immediately more comfortable, and I'd jump up on the front bench seat, put my hands on the dash, and look out to the ocean and sky over the harbor, to the islands hovering out there like clouds. It was always warm, with sun in the afternoon, and he'd have the window down and the radio on, Julie London or June Christy, some big-band arrangement. He'd be tapping along with the beat, hitting the bottom of his big gold college ring on one of the three chrome bands around the green plastic steering wheel. Sometimes he'd whistle along or sing; sometimes he'd light up a Philip Morris.

The rich light of afternoon spread across the wide windshield like sawdust as I sat there looking out to the blue curve of the earth for as long as I could, thinking my hazy thoughts, knowing we lived out there, by the beach. The road wound down the hill, and near town the eucalyptus and jacarandas took up most of the sky. I was happy heading for Humphrey Road and home, the salt air blowing up from Miramar Point—I think we both were happy then.

He'd drop me off, and another day's ordeal was over. Our house was the yellow one in back of the grey one near the street where our landlady lived—Auntie Doris I came to call her. She watched after me afternoons, made me peanut butter and honey sandwiches, and showed me again and again the Marine memorabilia of her dead husband, Elmo. More than anything, I liked his little uniform collar pins, the world with an anchor through it.

I knew where I was, where I wanted to be, living among the camphor trees a block from the beach. The sycamores in the yard had leaves the size of dinner plates; the pyracantha bushes beneath the window fed the mockingbirds. Across the creek in back, there was a large field of grain and a lemon orchard on the Hammond estate. I never asked about Dorothy and where exactly she lived. I was committed to the blue Technicolor sky in my eyes all weekend, when I would not have to take naps and could run freely through the bright and untroubled light of home.

STARRY AMBITION

My father's gypsy heart skimmed just beneath the surface of success. One enterprise to the next, one town to the next, one house to the next, he arrived looking like he owned it all, in his knit tie and Florsheim shoes, his sport jackets and college ring. And from college to network broadcasting, from his own radio station to real estate, the design was vague, but grand, and glowed like the sun over the vast Pacific.

Yet it must have been more difficult, finally, to fail, to not cash in big, than it was to succeed, as the opportunities of the '50s and '60s were legion. Given the houses and land he owned early on, the appreciation of values between the '50s and the '90s, there must have been some streak of stubbornness, some black luck or bad star, some flaw that firmly opposed him to fortune, blindsided him financially time and again, and so kept him from becoming the King of Montecito. Living in this backwoods suburb of Santa Barbara, it took me half my life to figure out what he really wanted.

We rubbed elbows with the rich—our one acre to their many—but we owned an acre those early days in a place where prices now run true to the cliché, "If you have to ask, you can't afford it." By any measure, we owned modest homes, but by simply being there, the foothills, oaks, and creeks, the secluded blue expanse of sky and bright air were equally ours. But something wouldn't let him hold still. He had to make deals. He sold the houses, invested in businesses, bought other houses, rented, leased, traded up, down, and sideways until he lost out. He kept on the move, and at the end of his life he owned nothing and paid skyrocketing rents despite forty years of opportunity to make a killing by just holding on to one place, one time.

No, there was always the next opportunity, the next better deal, and he was happy to spell out the advantages of the new this over the old and familiar that. "A wealth of opportunity," he always said—the wealth realized only in the number of opportunities and never in the results. Looking back at it now, I see it was the overall montage of commerce in the world, that self-congratulatory glow of merchants greeting each other on the street, outside the coffee shops or dry cleaners, that attracted and halfway contented him, satisfied and confirmed the relative importance of his life.

Yet he was not, it seemed, obsessed with any vocation or singular career, although he was for many years connected with music and broadcasting. He enjoyed, as far as I could tell, just being in business, the image it allowed him to uphold and project. Each morning he prepared to meet the world, snapping gold cuff links into place and staves into the collars of his starched and laundered shirts; he gave his cordovan wingtips six perfunctory back and forth swishes with a horsehair brush; he splashed on Old Spice aftershave. The jobs changed, the ritual never did.

Before, and for a little while after, the war he sang with big bands, and from the little I discovered about his life, I think that beyond the singing, his self-image as a crooner, his life was all a slow disappointment. All he really wanted, I came to see—down deep, deeper than he would ever say even to himself—was the casual comfort, the glow and easy glamour of a song. He wore the same stylish suits, stood in the same burning lights a while, and knew the adulation that went to Crosby, Haymes, or Sinatra all their lives. His ambition was, I finally think, to be a Star.

He failed at that, or fate failed him. I never knew. Finding out about my father's life, his true goals and desires, was much like astronomy—slowly, year by year, reading a little more into the thin stream of light particles dusting down from the dark, putting quanta together for information as best you can until one day the light stops arriving altogether, and you're left with a pinpoint fixed against the night.

As a child, I knew he could sing, heard his baritone slide right along with Perry Como ("Don't let the stars get in your eyes...") or harmonize slowly with Rosemary Clooney ("Hey there, you with the stars in your eyes..."). He regularly made pronouncements about who on radio or TV really had a voice. Gordon MacRae could sing, Johnny Mathis was all gimmick. Thirty years later, after a dinner of chicken and vegetables and his one glass of chilled Mogan David concord wine, I got a little out of him about how he used to sing with bands, how he probably "could have really been someone" if he'd stayed with singing. The one bright moment from his youth I ever heard him recall was from his sophomore year in high school, a Saturday afternoon packed into a theater in Columbus, Ohio, to hear Judy Garland sing. At the beginning of a torch song, she left the stage and walked down the center aisle along the front rows, stopped and sat in my father's lap, placed both her arms around his neck, and sang to him for two or three bars. No doubt a regular part of her performance and routine, and he just happened to be a well-dressed boy with an aisle seat. Yet, all that time later, I could see he still felt it was about him—once he had been that close, the stardust on his lapel.

But what went wrong? He was pulled out of college and into the air cadets. After the war he was determined to finish school, find a job. Always so well turned out, he could pick up a salesman's position in any men's clothing store in any town he was in, but that was only a stopgap; other things were on his mind. He moved from one college to the next, working radio at the same time. He picked up assignments for "remotes," live broadcasts from big-band dances. Microphones that looked like Saturn with their metal rings stood on stage or sat on his small broadcasting table at the Meadowbrook in New Jersey—a crush of ten thousand to dance and hear Claude Thornhill. He was working near Cincinnati, enrolled in a drama school run by Tyrone Power's aunt, who told him his voice was better than Bing's. He'd known that all along.

He became sidetracked with the jobs while still determined to finish his college degree. Eight years, and he finally had his BA from Humboldt State in northern California, one of the few places offering a major in broadcast communications. But he kept working as a DJ across the country, station to station: Charleston, West Virginia, Springfield, Missouri, until we came to Santa Barbara on the coast of southern California. He worked for years at various stations in town, joined the Chamber of Commerce, borrowed a little, started a sound-wiring company, acquired the franchise for Muzak, sold that and built his own FM station. In the early '60s Goldwater and the far right agenda overtook his focus on time and life. He poured through daily copies of the *Congressional Record* and read from it on the air to alert us to communism, liberals, and dupes. He kept pitching the commercial spots, however, and made a going concern of his station before selling it for less than half of what it was worth and moving to Arizona. Another move I never understood. We never talked much those years except for me to hear his political views. Doing business was everything, seven days a week. Yet somehow, he always needed money and finally had to sell the radio station. All I knew then was that he was retiring for a while. In Scottsdale, he built a fabulous two-story house with a pool, Spanish tiles, the works—then ran out of money and had to sell that at a loss and return to work.

He wanted to have the marks of success that good business provided. How you arrived and got around was important. As far back as 1945, cars were a focus for him, a personal emblem. My mother's life insurance money from the death of her first husband bought them a new and hard-to-get Pontiac right after the war. She and her sister ordered it from Cincinnati and drove in from a small town in Kentucky to pick it up when it was ready. Any new car then was status, but this wide, cream-colored v-8 was something. They could have put a big down payment on a house, but it was the car, the gloss and prestige he wanted. Always he had the expensive models, and while he never owned a Ferrari or Lotus Esprit Turbo, he did have upscale autos, and often two, leased with large payments and huge insurance rates. He owned a limited production Triumph, the Stag, and sold it after a few years. Two years later, he bought it back from the person he sold it to and dumped over $10,000 into it for reconditioning and improvements. He kept it another two years, took it to concourse shows, and then, when money became a bit tighter, sold it for much less than he had put into it.

During these years, the last ten or so of his life, he had moved back to Santa Barbara and gone into real estate, commercial properties, and ranches, big-ticket items, and for several years running was the top salesman in the company. The first year he received a cheap pocket watch as recognition; the years following, a cruise along the Mexican coast for a week. He did so well for a while that he was able to make a deal with the company to keep a higher percentage of the commission than anyone else in the business. To his credit, he was entirely honest and aboveboard in his business dealings—this probably contributed to his failure later on, as other salesmen in the office stole his leads and managers shaved his commissions. But before the last lean years, I could not figure where the money went—an income of over $100,000 a year for several years? Even a bad investment, like the land he bought in Missouri, could not have eaten up such money. As a getaway from natural disaster or invasion by the communists, he figured this undeveloped land near the Ozarks was worth paying on. No wells, no access roads, no nothing near by. After his death, despite the down payment and years of regular monthly payments, that land was not worth the amount left owing on the loan. All that time, he could have bought land or houses in Montecito or Santa Barbara. The value went up every year, even in the '80s when prices were already high—he could have made a bundle in five or six years, but he just kept paying high rent for a three-bedroom condo. One room was filled with nothing but shoes, tweed sport coats, shirts, and slacks. And there were always two halfway exotic Japanese sports cars in the garage, on lease. But where could the money have gone—did that take it all? He and my stepmother took no trips, ate out very modestly only once a week, and did not drink.

The last three years of his life nothing closed. Escrows he worked on for six months or more canceled at the last minute, several of them. He and Nancy invaded their mutual funds and IRAs, and Nancy had only been able to persuade him to start contributing to them a few years before. No life insurance either—he would live forever.

When he died suddenly, Nancy had a $1,300-a-month rent and about $1,500 going out each month on two car lease payments and insurance. She called the banks to explain Bill had died, and she could not keep the leases, but the banks were not interested in the extenuating circumstances of death—she was told to pay or they would sue. Business was business—imagine that? But one deal closed just after he died, and Nancy had enough to pay off hospitals, unscrupulous doctors, and leases, and enough to live on for almost a year. There was nothing else. A life of work and apparently unmitigated ambition for business had amounted to this, had proved nothing as its reward.

Well before I was out of my twenties, I had decided not to go that route. My father's ambition for me was as veiled, as skewed as his own goals. As a child I knew I would go to college long before I had any clear idea what a "college" was. My father repeated this often—it was a middle-class point of honor, of class, and of self respect, I later came to see. I was told—anyone in the room was told—as far back as I can remember that I would go to college, and, when I went, I would wear polished cotton trousers, loafers, a nice tie, and a sport jacket. I would look the part. My mother once told me that when my father was attending Humboldt State he would arrive on campus wearing his camel-hair sport coat and knit tie, slacks and wingtips, and students would stop him, thinking he was a professor, and ask information. The idea of it, the outward manifestation concerned him, satisfied his ambition for me, it seemed, more than the eventual reality. But soon, by the mid '50s, I heard less about college—the benchmark of middle-class success after the war—and more about my tennis. He was determined I would become a world-class tennis player. I did well at it from as early as six years old through high school, when his constant pushing and my discovery of surfing dissipated any permanent interest or achievement.

Later, in graduate school, I came back to tennis—teaching, playing local tournaments—and I could see some spark of hope resurrect itself in his eyes. The fact that I had taken my college degree and was at work on a second graduate degree didn't impress him; it never came up in conversation. Perhaps the fact that I switched in college from business administration to English had some effect? As a boy, when he took me to L.A. for the Notre Dame vs. USC football games, he would always go through the programs pointing out how many of Notre Dame's players were business administration majors compared to all the physical education majors for USC. But that was long ago. I think more and more he remembered himself still standing on the stage in front of a microphone, catching the cue from the trombone and leading into "Serenade in Blue" or "Street of Dreams." Sad as it is, he had to know then, late in his sixties, that it would have meant more to follow his first love of singing, no matter how insubstantial the rewards. Still, he'd talk about my promise and abilities as a tennis player to anyone who'd listen, and, although later I'd taken graduate degrees and was getting by teaching, writing, and publishing books, he'd lament how I'd "ruined my career."

In 1980, I was moving back to Santa Barbara, taking a job at the university there, and playing a little tennis again to keep in shape. In those days he had his cars and had just bought a $9,000 Rolex, a watch worth easily three times as much as my Ford Fiesta. Then he would proclaim to me the virtues of real estate, how I ought to quit teaching and take up selling houses, as many teachers had. Ambition ran in one direction for him. It was concrete and material and was manifest in Rolexes and cars—it manifested itself in status. These were things worth having. Teaching as a vocation, a profession, was never discussed. He didn't see it. I drove a small economy model, several years old, after all. What was it all going to come to for me anyway?

As a child, one of the few things I knew about him was that he kept a book of Shakespeare's plays and a copy of *Leaves of Grass* in his one box of memorabilia in the garage. I never saw him take either out and read; they were more like souvenirs from a vacation in lost and distant lands, much like the large red star he kept in the same box, which a Russian pilot had taken off his cap and given to him during the second war. He had no idea that Whitman was homosexual, and beyond the usual run of clichés from Hamlet, I had no specific notion why he admired Shakespeare other than it was drama and he had studied some acting when young. He spoke about these things rarely, wistfully, cryptically—the mysteries of the stars reflected in the blades of grass, other life beyond our solar system, the unknown drama of the universe, and the apparent insignificance of our lives. These wistful excursions into a self-made metaphysics—often offered up walking to or from the car beneath the still, clear firmament over southern California in the '50s and '60s—surely belied the eighty-hour work weeks he put in and the high seriousness of a dollar.

We never talked about my writing. The only poem of mine we ever discussed was one for which I pumped him for information. Long after graduate school, Nancy had clued me into stories about his Air Force time flying between Egypt and South America, about unknowingly swimming in the barracuda-infested waters in Takerati Bay off the coast of Africa. He had been transported on a liberty ship—the *John C. Calhoun*, he remembered—that zigzagged for over forty days avoiding u-boats on the way to Africa. At night, barely moving at four knots over the dark sea, with all those servicemen on the deck, no one was allowed to smoke—they were running dark to avoid detection. Every now and then they saw a ship get hit, going up, a flare like a match struck on the far horizon. Once they arrived, he and Howard jumped from the ship and swam all the way around it before finding out about the barracudas. Later, he and Howard, his one friend in the war and in life it seemed, had piloted their DC-3 from Egypt to South America, stopping on a speck of rock—Ascension Island—in the Atlantic to refuel, a spot many missed. Good stories, and the poem used them. I gave him a copy of the journal that published the poem, but he never mentioned it. The evening I asked about it, he had just put on a remastered record of Artie Shaw and a young Mel Torme, and I could see as he listened that all he really wanted to remember were those starry evenings singing with a band.

Yet he kept suggesting I take the real estate course, pass the test for my license, so at least in the summers I could "sit" on houses for him, make some money, see about a real estate career first hand. He never came over to the little place I was living in then—a small California bungalow that a stepbrother had bought and was fixing up. There, I rented a bedroom that looked out on a large pasture with tamarisks, cactus, agaves, and one dusty white horse that wandered around in the weeds. I decided to spend my summer at a desk staring out that window. I had next to no money, no savings, and all I had to show for my work that year at the university was a reconditioned electric typewriter and two new Hawaiian shirts for summer. Both bolstered my spirits enough to get by month to month just writing.

But perhaps I'd learned something, if only unconsciously, as my ambition did not reach beyond the blue evening sky above the yucca blossoms and trumpet vines, the dull yellow meadowlarks that scrounged the field in the grey light of dusk. I became content just listening to the wind's small music in the green needles of tamarisk. I wanted to hold the light impounded in the feathery plumes of pampas grass wavering up the hill toward the campanile. Each evening, I liked to stand out there in my favorite shirt, the one with a few coconut palms and outriggers in a breeze, a breeze that allowed me to stay with the thing I loved, there in one place. Some cabbage roses volunteered along the garage, the jade plants glistened richly with water from the hose. Whatever the outcome, when I looked back to this moment, it would at least be clear I had not sold out, that I still had a hold on my life and, for better or worse, on my one ambition. I was free and irresponsible enough to do what I wanted beneath the indeterminate skies—empty-handed in the dark, except for the stars.

HISTORY OF MY HAIR

Hair. In the late '50s and early '60s, it was about all you had. All the consumerism and conspicuous consumption—Ronald Reagan and his always perfect conservative hair—were decades in the future. You were a kid, you wanted to be cool, you had a comb and a little grease, and you made the best of it. There were no designer names, few brand names, and, especially if you attended a parochial school, everyone looked the same. Except for their hair. You could be as cool, as way-out as your hair. It was a democracy of sorts for youth—an equal opportunity for radicalization on the smallest scale. But to buck the "I like Ike" society, its lack of hair and imagination—its Robert B. Hall and J.C. Penney simple-suit view of the world—was difficult to do. Hair was, as it always has been, a source of vanity, but it was then the one possible way to be yourself, to be "with it," and it was the way to be.

1955, and my first day in a new school a kid comes up to me before class and says over his shoulder to a friend, "I wonder what this new kid looks like when he cries." I barely had a second for his salami-breath and crooked nose to register before he sucker punched me in the stomach. As I was doubling over, I noticed his hair—just a kid, and he had it combed like some hot-rodder in one of those early teen-hoodlum movies; it was wiry and obviously held in place by Butch Wax, an application so thick that it glistened like lard as the sun struck the side of his head. The top was combed straight forward, tight wings flared back along the sides, and the front worked to a small spit curl in the center of his forehead—a wave working from each side to meet and crash in the middle. G.G. Colson was a "tough," as I immediately learned from his right uppercut and from the fact that he dared the nuns with a hairstyle that was basically forbidden.

The kid who called him off after one punch and who later became my friend, Tuck Schneider, also risked a similar waterfall effect and flat-combed top a little later, in fifth grade. By then, we had all the examples we were ever going to need, every one our parents wished we'd never had. Freddy Cannon, Bobby Rydell, Fabian, and Eddie Cochran appeared in movies and on Dick Clark's *American Bandstand* with their huge jelly rolls, a wave in the front at least three inches high. Elvis had arrived on TV's *The Ed Sullivan Show* and taken it a step further than that big wave in the front rolling back in grease; he'd combed the sides back until they met in the back of his head. This was called a ducktail; this was going too far for the parents and self-appointed moral guardians of society then. On that first *Ed Sullivan Show* the censors had directed the cameras to cut Elvis off at the waist and so avoid his wiggling hips and knees—they had to show the hair! We didn't know much—fashion was not infused into every inch of the media, into the middle and lower middle class as it is now. Just pick up any of the calendars or photo books on Elvis and look at the clothes he was wearing in the '50s and '60s—awful stuff—but so were everyone else's, and no one was looking at the clothes. As kids, we knew uniforms, suits, and blue jeans, with jeans not being allowed at school, restaurants, church, etc. Otherwise, we didn't take much notice. Everyone seemed to have roughly the same gear. There were only two or three brands of tennis shoes, all black high-tops, and they all cost about $2.00. But if you maneuvered your hair into a ducktail as Tuck Schneider's older brother Joe did, you got noticed. Noticed enough to get suspended from Santa Barbara Public High School, a place those of us in Catholic school saw as a bastion of liberal thinking. After three days Joe recombed his hair so the wings on the side of his head did not flare up too much and so they did not meet in the back of his head and returned to school and some modest celebrity. One day after school at Tuck's house, with no one home, we both stood in front of the tall mirror in his brother's room and tried to comb our hair into ducktails; Tuck's did not work, as he had slightly curly hair, but mine worked perfectly, as I already had the wave in front and my hair was straight. Tuck encouraged me to leave it like that, but I didn't have near the nerve. We saw Joe as a minor hero—his hair, just a shade lighter, was exactly like Elvis's. And of course the first thing he did after school, as soon as the first foot touched the public sidewalk on Anapamu or Milpas Street, was to pull out his comb and put the doo-wop back in the wings and rolls there—the Brylcreem, Butch Wax, or Wildroot Cream Oil more than adequate to accommodate the more radical remodeled coif as he stepped out into the world on his own.

One day at the end of lunch period, Schneider, Colson, Fisher, Knapp, Sozzi, and I were all in front of the mirrors in the washroom, and we decided, no doubt at Colson's instigation, to comb our hair like rock 'n' roll stars. Colson combed the side wings of his springy hair forward with a ducktail in the back, something no one had ever done—or would want to do—so far as we knew. A few went for the waterfall spit curl, and forward-combed the top. Sozzi and I tried for the Jimmy Dean style with the jelly-roll wave and high sides winging back—hard to tell from Elvis's really. In we went when the bell rang, thinking we were "really gone" and drawing lots of looks from our classmates. Right out we went as soon as Mrs. Hansen saw us. We would go back to the washroom and comb our hair "properly," or she'd call in the principal, Sister Vincent de Paul. VDP we knew would suspend us. Lucky for us, Mrs. Hansen was a layperson, as we called them then. Oh, we realized we'd gone too far, but we thought we were somebody for three or four minutes.

For some reason the small moves teens made toward independence with a few hairstyles was viewed as downright immoral—as was the music in general, of course, the hair guilty as emblem and by association. We returned to Mrs. Hansen's history class with our hair parted properly on the side and modest waves in the front like every Junior Chamber of Commerce man and his son and sat there quietly waiting for our graduation, when we thought we'd be able to wear our hair however we wanted. We'd seen some movies, some posters or clips on TV, seen James Dean or Elvis or Fabian just stop in the middle of what they were doing, spread their feet apart for balance, reach to their back pockets for their combs as smoothly as some gunfighter in a western reaching for his gun, and recomb and shape their hair before continuing. There was flare to the move—the comb was whisked out and two or three full strokes front to back applied; a small shake of the shoulders and adjustment of the shirt sleeves, then an almost existential (if we'd known that word then) gaze in the eyes was also required. We mimicked this in no time, but only those at the top of the social pecking order could get away with it; those further down or with less flagrant styles were razzed when they tried the same moves.

After the summer, a couple of our friends came to school with flattops—the newest thing and a style that skirted the taboos as it was essentially a crew cut, the hair cut down to a half inch evenly on the top, but it left the sides and back long enough to comb back into "fenders." High schoolers and hot-rodders left the very front of the flattop long so they could comb it toward the middle of their foreheads into a dangling spit curl. Younger kids had the front only slightly longer than the buzzed top and just had it stick straight up and spiky. Lots of the flattoppers carried a little bottle of Butch Wax that came with a comb that you replaced in the bottle after you used it, but its popularity didn't last long as it didn't stay closed and so was a very messy proposition. My father absolutely forbid me a flattop, and in the summers my mother always argued for a crew cut, the universal buzz.

Only when your parents weren't paying attention, which wasn't often, could you comb your hair in the current fashion and thereby be somebody to yourself and your peers. My father was always after me to comb my hair like his, straight back, no grease. He would only barely sanction the average-middle-American part on the side. I should—and someday he just knew I'd have the sense to—wear my hair straight back; somehow, that was the only acceptable and moral style. It was serious business then, how you wore your hair—people cared, noticed. Each morning I rubbed enough Wildroot Cream Oil into my hair that it would hold whatever shape I refigured it to once at school. I then went mainly for the wings along the side and a large Fabian-tall wave in front. I had lots of hair and enough hair oil to be at the top of the fashion in my school group.

But in no time the '50s, which had hung on into the early '60s, were gone. Sure Elvis was still Elvis, but surfing had come on, was popular in movies and music, and, for some, as an actual sport. But popular culture soon had Elvis and Fabian with their shiny hair completely in place riding twenty-foot waves at Sunset Beach in Hawaii or shooting the pier at Huntington Beach. I'd learned to surf and had been out on some big waves—it didn't take much experience to know how phony those Elvis surf films were with him standing in the middle of a board, feet parallel like a rank beginner, a studio fan blowing in his face and perhaps only two or three strands of his ducktail out of place. No real surfers ever went to those films. And then there were the "hodaddies"—"hodads" for short—guys with greasy hair who drove around with boards in or on their cars to parties, or to the surf spots, guys who never went out into the surf.

Right then, what you wanted for the surfer look was dry, shaggy hair, and by all means blond. That left me out on most counts. And for the first year or so I was surfing, ages thirteen and fourteen, I was in a boys' boarding school where you still had to have a short cut and pass inspection for dinner—suit and tie, shoes shined, hair slicked into place. I'd quit the vo5 and thicker greases that were still fairly popular in the early '60s. I'd gone over to Vitalis, a more watery application, which, after it dried, left your hair stiff and certainly in place. One friend at that school, Joe Lubin (a liberal user of vo5), invited me home to his house in Beverly Hills for a weekend; it seemed there was a party with a number of his friends, and he had a date for me, a really cute girl he said. So we showed up in sport coats, ties, and slacks (the Beatles and the rest of the early "British invasion" of rock 'n' rollers would still dress that way in the years right ahead) and met our dates. I could see that Joe was there to meet his girlfriend, and they went off immediately to the dance floor and glued themselves together. My date was indeed as attractive as promised, but she wanted nothing to do with me. I thought perhaps it was because I wasn't from her school. But later in the evening I heard from Joe that the problem was my hair! He had promised her a date with a surfer, and although she herself did not surf, she knew that "surfers" did not have black hair like mine. We were introduced and that was basically the last I saw of her. I sat by myself for a while, knowing no one there except Joe, who was still leaning into his date on the dance floor. Finally, one of the cheerleaders came over and asked me to dance; she hung around and talked a while as well. Obviously a more mature woman, she still appreciated the hairstyles and look of the '50s!

But I could see something had to be done. Here I was, a real surfer with an appropriately beat-up Yater surfboard and surf knots on my knees, but I did not look the part. That summer I tried the lemon routine. A surfing friend told me that another guy we knew, Don Bullock, had actually gotten his dark hair to turn blond by putting lemon on it and staying in the sun for a few hours. We saw Don at one of the beaches and he had this slim streak of light red in the front, miles from blond. Nevertheless, I tried it, but the lemon thing never worked. Lots of kids were trying the peroxide route, which I never did; you could always tell those who had; their hair had a very artificial orange tint. I just went for the surfing and forgot about my hair for a while; besides, my friend and the best surfer in the area, Harry Fowler, had coal-black hair, so—so what?

Grease was gone, and if you surfed, you just combed your hair once in a while and let it be as dry and floppy as possible. There were unofficial dress codes in high school, although there were no uniforms. The Beatles hit in 1963–64, and I can remember thinking how radically long their hair was in that picture on the cover of their album. Look at that now and John, Paul, George, and Ringo look as if they have very respectable cuts. Of course the late '60s and '70s came with truly long hair for everyone, but then just a touch over the ears with bangs in the front was radical rock 'n' roll communist-hippiedom! My friend Francis Orsua—who to this day has a thick mop of hair—and I skipped a few haircuts and cultivated the Beatles' look. Orsua even got his picture taken and put in the local *Santa Barbara News Press*—he was just walking down State Street and a newspaper photographer, out to capture a newsworthy fringe element loose on our streets, took a photo of Orsua with his hair over his collar. Mine was not so long, but without any hair oil that huge wave of a couple years previous now fell across my forehead, and I had bangs easily as long as Paul McCartney's, or so some girls I knew had told me. On a Friday after school, the disciplinarian, Father Bernard, called Orsua and me over from our lockers and, without argument or complaint, told us to be sure and see a barber at the weekend or not bother coming to school Monday. What could we do? We got it cut and lost what little notoriety we'd achieved.

For the girls then, length of hair was not such a critical factor—long or short, any style was acceptable. Many wore a variation on the pageboy, shoulder-length hair with bangs. However, when there was a dance, they had to spend hours torturing their hair up into a beehive, a style that made the tops of their heads look like a funnel of cotton candy. Lacquered and sprayed into form, they predated the coneheads by many years; it was brittle and hard at the same time, but for formal occasions, it was the style. Some girls back-combed or "ratted" their hair to make it poof up and stay poofed, to accommodate the beehive look beyond the parameters of a dance. There was Gilda Bedola, who always had the biggest blond hair at school, and though she was an inveterate ratter she was plenty attractive. She only dated boys from the public high school though, and whenever we saw her someone always brought up the story of the girl who never took down her ratted beehive and who was finally killed by black widows that built a nest in there. Surely an apocryphal story since people at so many different schools knew it. But it says something about the senselessness of style in the first place—what we will put up with or aspire to in judging one look better than another.

I went off to college in northern California and within a year or so Orsua went into the Marines, and that was the end of hair considerations for us both. Orsua just wasn't allowed to have any, full stop, and I had too many things to worry about as a freshman at St. Mary's College, in Moraga, California. Ours was the last freshman class to be hazed—systematically humiliated and tortured by older students. In the past, many freshmen had their heads shaved and painted, but in our class that only happened to one or two. We spent time sneaking around, trying not to be apprehended by upperclasssmen. There were studies, sports, work on weekends, and just too many people and pressures to worry about hairstyle then; I just got it cut once in a while in the campus barber shop and didn't think much about it. Didn't think much, that is, until our senior year, 1968–69, when some serious opposition to the Vietnam war started to arise nationwide. At our conservative, middle-class college, with a student body of about nine hundred, there were only fourteen or fifteen students openly opposed to the war, and only one student, in a class below us, had long hair; that was it, one guy in the whole school with some outward symbol of protest. I grew a mustache that year, but upon visiting my mother and stepfather on spring break had to shave it off, as my mother insisted that my stepfather would not stand for it—after all, he had been good enough to pick up the bills for college tuition after my father bailed out on the entire project. I shaved the mustache that night. How much was hair finally worth?

But the '70s were right around the corner. I took a teaching position at a Catholic school, grades seven and eight, right out of college. I had decided some time ago to teach, and I also hoped that I would receive a teaching deferment from the war. At Nativity Catholic School in Torrance, I met Doug Salem, the other new hire for seventh and eighth grades, someone who would become a wonderful and important friend to me until he died at age thirty-two in a car accident. On that first day of meetings before class we became instant friends. He had normal-length hair, but he also had long sideburns. As the year wore on and we both became involved in opposition to the war, saving the environment, and the next Crosby, Stills, Nash, and Young album, his hair became long and he wore striped Levis and looked the part of the counterculture. But he was brilliant, and his ideas on social justice and morality had a great effect on me. A few years later, still with his long hair, he would be appointed dean of a law school at the age of thirty-one. I decided to also grow my hair long then, though in truth it was nothing approaching the shoulder-length hairstyle that would become common in only another year or so. The length of our hair became a problem; parents at Nativity (Torrance was home of the largest Armed Forces Day parade in the country) were holding meetings, calling Doug and I communists (I had played a Bob Dylan record in class!). By the end of the year neither of us wanted to return.

Doug headed for law school, and I took a job teaching the same grades at a Catholic school in Santa Barbara—Our Lady of Mt. Carmel, the same school where G. G. Colson had stood there in his hot-rod hair and punched me out fifteen years before. When I went to see the principal—who really wanted a male teacher for the upper grades, for discipline, and for coaching sports—she said the job was mine but I would have to cut my hair; after all, the students were not allowed to have long hair. I pointed out that I was not a student and had just had it cut the day before the interview. Either way, I needed a job and would have to keep it short. When I called a few weeks later about books, contracts, and so forth, I was told that I no longer had the job. I could not teach any math, and the teacher who had agreed to teach the seventh- and eighth-grade math classes in trade for fifth- and sixth-grade English had backed out of the deal. I suggested that maybe she should lose her job as it was she who had broken the agreement, but she lived with another woman who taught at the school, and if one were fired the other had threatened to quit. So, goodbye.

I had one month's rent money left and had to find a job pronto. The only thing available to me at the last minute was the grocery store chain for which I worked in high school and during summers in college. I saw the personnel manager, said nothing about my teaching experience and little about my education, and was told I could have a position at just about the lowest level, but first I needed to look at this chart she pulled out from the desk showing allowable grooming for employees, including those who were only going to make $2.50 an hour. If I had a haircut, I could report to my old store on Milpas Street on Monday morning and start mopping and carrying out groceries. I went to see my friend Billy Bonilla, who was now a barber, and paid him what would be close to three hours' grocery wages to cut my hair.

Of course in the '70s, long hair became the norm. TV news anchors, sports announcers, politicians and preachers, everyone and anyone had longer hair. I couldn't see how some baseball players kept their uniform caps on, and many didn't as soon as they moved to make a play. Coast to coast, we had the stage production *Hair,* and when something was very difficult or terrifying it was described as "hairy"; if an act required a lot of courage, the idiom had it that "it took a lot of hair" to do it. Go figure. Take out some photos from the '70s, and, if you can get past that truly bizarre Pirates of the Caribbean garb we all wore then, look at our hair. Long, stringy, stacked, frizzy, chunky, you name it. It was there in abundance. I went back to graduate school at San Diego State University and after that at the University of California at Irvine. While taking my degrees, I managed to make money in the summers teaching tennis, and so there was no need for me not to have my hair long, truly long. I wore headbands, I fit in; I went more or less unnoticed through the times. While staying at my father's house those summers in school, I could see that he was undergoing a hair transplant. Each evening he'd have to retire to the bedroom and put on this shower cap to cover an application of salves and medicines that went over these pencil point plugs of hair that had been cut into his scalp. What a pain, I thought, figuring I'd never have to worry about that—my hair still thick then and long in my late twenties.

I taught part time at a number of places after graduating from Irvine, longish hair not a problem to get the job. When Proposition 13 passed in California, colleges and community colleges had to cut their part-time teachers, and my stint as a freeway faculty between three of them in the area came to an end. I moved to Fresno, where it seemed I could pick up some adjunct English classes at the university, and I taught there for two years. In the middle of that time my class at St. Mary's College was holding a ten-year reunion, and I decided to attend. I was hitting thirty and thought it a good time to have a good professional cut, a bit shorter than I'd had it for the past number of years. This especially hit home when a student in one of my composition classes at Fresno State called to me after class—a good kid with a sense of humor, and somehow I knew he didn't want to know more about the comma splice. He caught up to me and said, "Hey, Mr. Buckley, you've got wavy hair." My hair has always been straight, and so I asked him what he meant, and he didn't miss a beat and replied, "It's wavin' goodbye!"

I went to this barber not far from my house, a shop I'd passed by a number of times. In back of the two chairs the shelves were full of gadgets, a microscope-type machine to examine your hair and hair roots, special massagers, charts, etc. The news was not good; my hair was starting to weaken and thin. I should keep it cut shorter, he said, and avail myself of several potions and processes that he offered. About all I did was pay for the cut and get out, but I could see that I needed now to have a shorter style as it was thinning out in the usual places—something I never thought would happen to me as my hair had always been so thick. Thirty years old and body betrayal had begun, and that was pretty much the end of any consideration about hair for me. Keep it short and neat and maybe no one would notice how much light was beginning to reflect off the old cranium. I certainly was not going to be one of those guys with a part just above the ear and strands stretching pathetically over the top toward the other side. Nor was I about to go through the cost and ignominy of transplants, though my father's had worked well enough. His hair had gone all white and the transplanted spots on top and in front were OK. However, they were not near as full as the sides, which he had combed into vast swanlike wings, TV-evangelist style. His hair in his sixties was much longer than mine in my thirties, and he probably had more of it. What could I do about that?

What does any of it finally mean? I own more hats than I ever have—I think of skin cancer, whereas I never did before. Rogaine has been over-the-counter for a long time, and last Christmas a friend—half out of concern and half as a joke—gave me a four-month supply of the generic brand she'd picked up with the price mismarked at a discount store. It was easy to apply, just topical—like a little alcohol—but three months later I couldn't see a strand of difference. But I don't know, another month and continued applications and it may stop the rapid retreat to the rear? Either way, I pass no moral judgments. By this point in time, I'm either content with who I am or I am not; it's a question of character finally. And health. A great lot of hair like Jim Carrey or Andy Garcia can't change things, won't make you feel any better about yourself—will it?

MY LIFE IN BOXING

Thwunk! Thwunk! Thwunk! Carlson's jabs landed square on my forehead before I knew—quite literally—what hit me. Two, maybe three, more lefts tattooed the crown of my head with a sound like someone stubbornly thumping a casaba melon, testing for ripeness—or emptiness?—a sound that ricocheted between my ears. Then a right cross caught me flat-footed, and both legs turned to jelly.

Twenty seconds into the bout and I had just enough sense left to hold both gloves up in front of my face, wrists outward, and wave them crisscrossing the air, signaling I'd had enough—more than enough. That "No más! No más!" gesture for which Roberto Duran became famous, or infamous, some twenty years later, he got it from me in sixth grade, 1959.

I stumbled up the stone steps from the priest's rectory to the faucet at the back of the garage, the one we always drank from coming off the playing field. As I bent down and turned my head under the spigot, face to the sky so the water could numb the ridge of pain welling up like a lobster shell on my forehead, I almost passed out. Looking up, I could feel the clouds above me floating around in the dizzy blue atmosphere of my brain. The water was not doing much for the crack I was sure had opened in my skull from my widow's peak down to the bridge of my nose, and I was just able to steady myself, hand on the spigot, and stand up.

How had I gotten into such a spot? "What in the world"—as my father always said—"had possessed me?" Especially with those ridiculous gloves—huge, overpadded red boxing gloves that looked like they came right out of the cartoons—gloves so huge Bluto could slip a horseshoe inside before hitting Popeye with a roundhouse hay-maker right. I felt like Popeye in that cartoon, before he ate the spinach—a crown of dark stars spinning over my head and two or three bluebirds tweeting repetitively out of tune.

For reasons never revealed to the sixth-grade boys at Our Lady of Mt. Carmel School, one spring lunch hour the pastor, Father Ozzias B. Cook, had marched us down into the rectory yard for boxing matches, with those gloves. I remember skinny Peter Cooney, the gloves weighing half as much as he did, paired off against his pal Harry Fowler. The idea was for pairs of equal size and weight, but no one was as light as Cooney, and Peter was not going to back out and look a coward, so he mustered all his energy and came at Harry, both hands flailing like an out of control windmill, and Harry just de-flected the blows. Schneider and Fisher, Knapp and Stanton Richards, Wesley and Wytucki—no bouts lasted more than a minute and a half as everyone's arms grew fatigued with the gloves, and no one had the least idea about proper punching technique or footwork.

It was all over, it seemed, until Carlson put on the gloves and Father Cook looked around for someone to match up against him. My first clue should have been that the gloves did not look quite so big on Carlson's arms, the second that none of the other boys volun-teered—everyone staring down at his shoes, or off into the sky above the bell tower of the church from where no angels were going to descend and save me.

Carlson was the biggest kid in the class, the best athlete. I was one of the next in size, and given the atmosphere of mindless bravado already in the air, I puffed up my chest and said I would step into the makeshift ring with him. My boxing experience did not extend beyond a few school yard scuffles in earlier grades, which were mostly wrestling and rabbit punches. I knew little more than the correct stance—left foot forward, left glove up, and head tucked down into the right collarbone—something I'd picked up from Ingrid Bergman playing a nun in *The Bells of St. Mary's* as she taught a student how to stand up to the playground bully. What I really didn't know, and what really hurt me, was that Carlson had been taking boxing lessons at the YMCA, a fact he casually revealed later that day. Size would have counted on the football field, equaled out on a blocking assignment, but nothing made up for an educated looping left hook.

I don't think Father Cook knew that Carlson had studied the "manly art of self-defense." More than likely, the good pastor was just trying to make us look foolish to ourselves and point out the futility of fighting, and he might have succeeded in putting his point across had Carlson not given an effective exhibition of power and accuracy that made the other boys admire him and his skills all the more. As the one brave (stupid?) enough to mix it up with Carlson, I received some pats on the back from friends, but that was a hard way to move up the social ladder at school. What could I possibly have been thinking? I knew from nothing, and what little I did know had just about been beaten out of me.

What twist of imagination led me to believe I could simply assume a crouch, push a glove forward, and it would all turn out OK? What motivated the priest to round up a bunch of essentially mild-mannered Catholic boys into an impromptu fight club? Everything, it seemed, we had seen so far.

I had never seen a real live boxing match. My father had never taken me down off lower State Street to the big warehouse/local fight club my friend Orsua told me about. Boxers from Santa Maria or Oxnard or Ventura would drive up in a couple cars to Santa Barbara for fully officiated and timed bouts of three, eight, or ten rounds. A regular crowd paid to get in, and Orsua's father and uncle Robert would go there and watch aspiring semi-amateur lightweights and welterweights, mostly guys who'd learned to box in the armed forces. Years later, in high school, I discovered that one of my classmates, Gary DeVito, had an uncle, Pat Hernandez, who had been one of the most well-regarded fighters there. Boxing was still such an ingrained part of the American social fabric that local fight clubs thrived throughout the '50s, but as it all became more commercial, as TV entered into it in a big way, such places disappeared, and the club facilities on Montecito and Quarantina streets became the Mission Linen building.

But early in the '50s I knew little about any of this. I had yet to even open the *Encyclopedia Britannica*, volume 3, "BALTIM to BRAIL," and discover the dark photograph of the arena during the Dempsey-Carpentier fight of 1921 in Jersey City. Gate receipts were $1,789,238.00, and there were about eighty thousand people in the audience. The photo shows a huge arena climbing up to the skyline—just a mass of black-and-white dots except for the men in the foreground of the photo, distinguished by their white straw boater hats. The only real contrast is the white sugar cube of a ring in the center. I was amazed that that many people would crowd in to see a fight. In the first part of the century, before income taxes, boxers made fortunes. Gene Tunney made almost $1 million from the second fight with Jack Dempsey, and Dempsey made close to $2.5 million in eight title bouts. Coming out of the depression, the country was fight-mad, and in 1945 Madison Square Garden had receipts of over $2 million. But taxes and TV caught up with the fight game. Heavyweight champ Joe Louis retired undefeated in 1949, his only loss to the IRS—the $2,722,000 Louis made in twenty-seven bouts was heavily taxed, and he took little into retirement. By 1955, when the ageless Archie Moore moved up a class and was floored by heavyweight champ Rocky Marciano in Yankee Stadium, it was the TV receipts that showed the biggest profit.

I had only seen fights on TV, but that, evidently, was enough to place me on the receiving end of Carlson's barrage of blows. I was living with our first-ever set, in 1955, and there were really only two sports for regular viewing—baseball and boxing, much more boxing than baseball, and though as kids we all were crazy for baseball, I saw plenty of boxing. Even late into the '50s, it was a national mania.

So there I was, extending my left arm beneath the weight of that huge glove, taking my first circling step to the left, figuring I would turn out to be no more inept than any of the other guys, with absolutely no skills but plenty of images of uppercuts and swift combinations imprinted in my brain. Sure, it was all reasonable, reasonable until the first five seconds in the ring had my head snapping back with a pain no imagination could manipulate.

There were no remotes; TVs had only a crunch control and thirteen channels (well, the channels went up to 13, but there was no channel 1), and your father decided what station you would watch. You saw boxing whether you liked it or not. Seven or eight years old, I didn't get it—you were sent to the principal's office for fights at school but this was OK? The real objection, however, for my friends and me to boxing was that it often came on opposite *Disneyland*. The *Gillette Cavalcade of Sports* was telecast on NBC and was essentially the Friday night fights, and *Disneyland* in those days was on Fridays too. All the kids then were crazy for the "Adventure Land" segments, which featured Davy Crockett in his coonskin cap fighting Indians and bears and beating up bunches of bad guys out on the frontier. Not only was there no politically correct sentiment in those days, we saw no parallel between Davy Crockett punching out a bunch of men and animals and boxing. Every boy I knew wanted a coonskin cap or a replica of the powder-loading musket he carried. A Davy Crockett feature-length movie was swarmed with kids one Saturday afternoon at the Granada Theater on State Street. Amazingly, Davy Crockett lived in my town, Santa Barbara. I of course didn't know the actor's, Fess Parker's, name—only Davy Crockett, and one night he was sitting only two tables away in Tiny's, the small Mexican restaurant on Milpas Street where we occasionally went. I could hardly eat my taco. Between 1954 and 1958 *Disneyland* was the first to offer a "miniseries," and most of the kids I knew grudgingly missed episodes on account of boxing.

So it was television that put the pictures in my mind—imagine that, even way back then. Looking back, I realize that I saw so many fights with my father that it seems as if they must have been on every other night. I remember the Gillette commercial jingle and the two high, quick dings of the ringside bell, the Gillette parrot saying something about, "To look sharp, and to feel sharp too…" There was no escaping it. During the spring and summer, there was usually one baseball game a weekend on TV. When we could find them, we'd watch reruns of *Home Run Derby* between Mickey Mantle and Harmon Killebrew, Ernie Banks and Hank Aaron, with no complaint.

Most of our channels were out of L.A.—5, 11, 9, and 13 were the independent, nonnetwork stations. One always had fights from the Olympic Auditorium in downtown L.A., with Jimmy Lennon announcing. Whenever we drove to L.A. and got off the 101-Hollywood Freeway, just past the big "Brew 102" sign, I could see the painting of the boxer on the side of the huge auditorium. Another channel, all weekend it seemed, carried the fights from Tijuana—flyweights and bantamweights going after each other in what looked like fast-forward motion. Sometimes I even watched jai alai, again from Mexico, just because it was the only thing on that wasn't boxing.

Actually, I remember a time when there was no TV in our house, or in anyone's, but by the time I was seven, we were on our second set. There had been something wrong with our first one—a Philco, I think—the one in the blond wood cabinet that the TV repairman kept coming over to fix, placing his mirror in front of the screen and adjusting things from behind, where all the dusty tubes glowed with orange strings in the center. He'd pass a large grey donutlike thing in front of the screen (a degauzer, I later learned, for magnetic adjustment) and turn things with a screwdriver, but it still had lots of snow and ghost images despite my father's many adjustments to the rabbit ears on top of the set in between almost every round, and if it wasn't razor blades going wobbly, it was the Hamms bear or the Pabst Blue Ribbon can.

Soon, though, we had a huge Magnavox—an all-mahogany cabinet taller than I was, which had two wood doors in front of the screen that clicked together; each had a metal ring handle you pulled open to watch the set. The set, the cabinet, took over the living room. My father was passionate about the fights, and if I wanted to watch TV at all those nights, if I wanted to stay up past my bedtime, I sat on the carpet next to the chair he'd pulled up to within five feet of the screen.

In no time, I could identify the fighters and run off the litany of names—Joey Giardello, a middleweight, Eddie Machen, a heavyweight, and Sugar Ray Robinson, who had moved up from welterweight to middleweight. I knew all the regular fighters, which ones were "punching bags" for fighters on their way up, which ones could bob and weave, stick and move, who could "dance," who had a knockout punch or a glass jaw. Before the main event, I had to endure the preliminary bouts, three-round matches between flyweights or boxers I'd never heard of, as my father would watch it all. For some reason, or lack of reason, I was allowed to watch all the boxing but was forbidden to watch Steve Reeves in *Superman* afternoons after school. My father had heard a news report about a kid who tied a towel around his neck and tried to fly out the second-story window of his house— after, of course, watching Steve Reeves in his tights and cape swoop around the skies. My father must have thought my grasp on reality was tenuous, had he ever used the word "tenuous." Nevertheless, he had no second thoughts about the effects of boxing.

Most nights I hoped my father's favorite boxer would knock out his opponent in the early rounds so I could switch to *Disneyland*, but it rarely happened, and after a time I came to admire the same boxers he did simply by continued exposure. I knew I was in for a long evening if Carl "Bobo" Olson was on the card, as he was slow and yet could go the distance, absorbing a lot of punishment. I picked up phrases almost unconsciously, phrases like "absorb a lot of punishment," which was uttered half in admiration. I came to like the names too: Zora Folley, Tiger Jones, Dick Tiger, and Spider Webb—so many sounding fierce and mysterious. I became part of that culture of fathers and uncles and young men for whom boxing was a real, if vicarious, part of their lives, for whom it unthinkingly held meaning and offered heroes who connected to a long tradition, who represented some shining, dark portions of their souls. For my father—a man who had never been in a fight in his life, who dressed in stiffly laundered shirts and cuff links and camel-hair sport jackets—this blood sport was part of some imagined moral demeanor. Inevitably, whoever was fighting that night against his chosen champ hit on the break, threw rabbit punches or low blows, and was never penalized as he should have been by the referee. He knew which fighters should win even if they didn't, which happened far too often for my father's view of things. He proclaimed when a blow had landed, or when it was blocked or only grazing. This was good versus evil, simple—and my father knew which was which. So I soon became aware of which fights were "fixed," and, based on my father's expostulations of the fight between rounds and after the decision, I learned a little about the crookedness of the fight game and a fair amount about its history.

The politics of boxing sunk in early, and it was more than my father throwing his hands up in the air and jumping from his chair when the infamous split decisions were announced. My father mentioned more than once that the Joe Louis–Max Schmeling fight should really have been won by Schmeling but that the sentiment against Germany due to the war had the fight awarded to Louis. I wasn't quite sure what he meant, as there were lots of photos of Schmeling on his back on the canvas, and Louis retired undefeated in 1949. Of course, that was before my time, even my early time as a kid in the '50s. However, I began to sense that something might not be all that fair in boxing as I watched a number of bouts with my father's favorite fighter, Sugar Ray Robinson.

Robinson was born in Detroit and learned to box in the same Brewster Gym where Joe Louis had learned. At age twenty, in 1940, he won the Golden Gloves. From repeated questioning of my father, I knew that winning the Golden Gloves meant you were an especially good amateur fighter and that the best pros had won them, a fact always announced at the beginning of the bouts. Sugar Ray's real name was Walker Smith; to this day I don't know how I know that. Moreover, I never heard why or how he changed to Sugar Ray Robinson, but it had to have something to do with his speed and footwork, his grace and tactical punching combinations. Truth is, I probably never saw Robinson at his best. He won the welterweight title in 1946 and the world middleweight crown on five separate occasions and retired, for the first time, in 1952. He had beaten "The Raging Bull," Jake La Motta, in 1945 in Chicago, and in 1952 was victorious over Bobo Olson and Rocky Graziano for the middleweight title. He then stepped up for a light-heavyweight title fight and defeated Joey Maxim. None of these fights were on TV. I did see a grainy black-and-white replay of Robinson's fight with Randolf Turpin at Earl's Court, London, in 1951. Turpin was aggressive, throwing short rights and left hooks, continually bobbing up and down, and Sugar Ray just couldn't find the range—his jabs and combinations merely taking out air over Turpin's head. The fight went the full fifteen rounds, and the decision was given to Turpin, who probably deserved it. In that fight, Robinson looked old, or slow and tired. Yet not long before he retired, in the rematch two months later, Sugar Ray knocked out Turpin in the tenth round.

Robinson started his comeback in late 1954 and lost to Tiger Jones on January 19, 1955, only his third bout returning from retirement. The first time I saw him on TV was one of his fights with Bobo Olson; in December 1955 he KO'd Olson in the second round, and in May 1956, on the rematch, he KO'd him in the fourth. It was, however, Robinson's fights with Gene Fullmer that first had me thinking that all, or at least some, of my father's complaints about the judging were legitimate. Fullmer was a tough customer to be sure, but it sure looked to us that Sugar Ray had easily out-pointed him in their first match, on January 2, 1957, in New York. The decision went to Fullmer, and this, of course, set up the rematch, which brought in more money. In May of that year in Chicago, Robinson knocked out Fullmer in the fifth round. Sugar Ray not only had grace and great skills, but he had grit and the ability to study an opponent, and rematches almost always went to him. This pattern could best be seen, even by the kid I then was, in Robinson's fights with Carmen Basilio, a fighter who was all rage and muscle and who was possessed of a mean left hook. I remember these fights better than any others I watched for several reasons: my father was more excited by the contest than at any time I could remember; the newspapers and TV and all the kids at school talked about the fights the way a World Series seventh game might be talked about; and after the second fight the cover of *Sports Illustrated* featured Basilio's face. The first title fight between Basilio and Sugar Ray was September 23, 1957, and the decision went to Basilio—a split decision, which my father always maintained was the sign of a fixed fight. Typically, the referee had Robinson ahead on points and/or rounds and gave the fight to him, but the two judges—usually from New Jersey, Chicago, or Las Vegas—scored the bout in favor of Basilio, or whoever opposed the fighter my father favored. Though he did rant and rave about the outcomes, it started to become a bit amazing to me that he could predict the judges' voting so accurately. In March of 1958 there was the rematch, which also went fifteen rounds; it was a "slugfest," a brutal fight. Robinson clearly won this brawl, and his face was swollen and bruised. It was, however, the photo on the cover of *Sports Illustrated* that marked my memory forever. Basilio was just too tough to knock out, too gutsy to quit. Sugar Ray continually landed combinations to the head, closing Basilio's left eye. In more modern times, they would have stopped the fight and awarded Robinson a TKO—a technical knockout—but there must have been too much money and interest in the fight to do so. My father was fairly jubilant when the bell sounded ending the fifteenth round, sure that even crooked judges could not give the fight to Basilio, and he was right. A few days later, a kid brought a copy of the *Sports Illustrated* to school with Basilio's face—or what was once his face—on the cover. In color, what you saw—and an image I cannot forget all this time later—was Basilio's eye, swollen purple in his head to the size of half a grapefruit; there was a slit in the middle of this empurpled balloon that looked like a cut with black stitches—that was the place where his eyelids and lashes had fused together. The rest of his face looked like a porterhouse steak in a car wreck. As kids, we thought it gory. And it was. How Basilio ever saw out of that eye again is something of a miracle.

There were two more fights between Sugar Ray and Basilio, which they split, and I missed them both. With my father, I saw the first Floyd Patterson and Ingemar Johansson heavyweight fight in 1959, in which Patterson, who never topped two hundred pounds, was TKO'd in the third round by Johansson's big right hand. I did not watch the two subsequent bouts in 1960 and 1961, which Patterson won. I had lost interest in seeing the fights, even if they were the only thing on TV in our house. Sugar Ray Robinson retired for good at age forty-four; the last time I saw him he had a small acting role on an episode of *Dragnet*, and he looked dapper in a pinstriped suit. That was about the end of the fight-life for me. I did not see the ex-con Sonny Liston clobber gentlemanly Floyd Patterson; I did not see Emile Griffith kill Benny Kid Parret. I remember walking through the living room one evening in 1962 when my father had Archie Moore's last world-class fight on the tube. Moore was forty-eight, and he was dropped cold by a youthful Cassius Clay in the fourth round. I thought it was pretty sad, and unfair.

HALF NOTES

Growing up, I never questioned why I knew the words to so many songs from my father's generation. To this day, I absentmindedly sing along with lyrics from '40s and even '30s tunes. Of course the radio was on all the time in the car, and, at home, the record player. By the time I was seven or eight, I'd heard a good deal of the popular music of the war era and after; I knew the bands and the vocalists, some by name. But there was a good part of the music I never heard.

Jazz. My father never used the word. He pledged his allegiance to the big bands and the singers of smoky ballads, and coming out of the '30s and '40s never recognized how the best of it held a thread that led all the way back to jazz, never it seemed, put his finger on the connection. Nevertheless, his business was music. He began young as a DJ, broadcasting the "remotes" from the dance halls where the big bands were playing. Sitting at a table, in front of him a giant radio microphone with its halo of rings, he'd cup a hand over his right ear and, in his low and melodious announcer's voice, tell the listening audience that he was, *Live at Frank Daily's Meadowbrook—coming up, Claude Thornhill and his orchestra with "Snowfall."*

Even early in college, he sang with bands. In his best coffee-colored suit and dark wavy hair, he would step up to the standing mike on cue and follow a trombone lead into "Blue Evening" or "Once in a While." He liked a little Benny Goodman, but Glenn Miller and Tommy Dorsey were more his style. Later, in the '50s, the Dorsey Brothers had a TV show and we tuned in every week. I was too young to understand the difference between the two—Jimmy with saxophone and swinging, upbeat tunes, Tommy more lyrical, professionally sentimental, and smooth. And during those years, the late '50s, when my father worked at most of the local radio stations in Santa Barbara, I remember him dismissing Stan Kenton and his orchestrations as "too far out." He seemed to have an almost political fervor about the music he played, who was or was not acceptable—Keely Smith but not Louie Prima, Sarah Vaughn but not so much Anita O'Day.

As a young man home from World War II he attended Schuster and Martin Dramatic School in Cincinnati, where Tyrone Power's aunt, who directed the school, told him his voice was better than Bing's. He met my mother there, my mother who had an excellent voice, who had been studying with Grace Raines, Doris Day's vocal coach. But it was his voice that counted then, and my mother's aspirations were put to the side. A crooner, that's what he wanted to be, that's what everyone who sang should be. But he hadn't done his homework, had not listened to the jazz recordings Bing made in the '30s—his fine scat singing, beginning with the Rhythm Boys in 1926. In his biography, *Call Me Lucky*, Bing Crosby wrote: "Every man who sees one of my movies or listens to my records or who hears me on the radio believes firmly that he sings as well as I do." As far as I could tell, though, my father really could sing. Was he star material? He never stayed with it long enough to find out. He knew only the smooth movie-star songs, the romantic leading-man numbers, and he saw himself in movies, I think, not in nightclubs.

I don't know what he did with Duke Ellington, how he could ignore his deeply emotional melodies and the sophistication of his arrangements and lyrics, but he did. He loved Ella Fitzgerald, but only when she sang ballads, evergreens, not the "sock" songs with the fast tempos or her scat improvisations. He came through the '50s spinning Frank Sinatra, Julie London, June Christy, and Gordon McRae—now *he* had a voice. To his credit, he played Sinatra at a time in the '50s when most DJs would not. The public had become disenchanted with Frank over the Ava Gardner affair and any number of things, but my father took no high moral ground when it came to a voice like that. At times, he went back to the old Tommy Dorsey recordings of Sinatra with Jo Stafford, Connie Hines, and the Pied Pipers—"Street of Dreams" and "Once in a While." At home, at age eleven or twelve and alone in the afternoon, I'd pull the little 33⅓ album from the cardboard jacket, the record with only four songs a side, and listen to Frank sing Cole Porter, again and again getting no kick from champagne, buying violets for your furs. A year later, I'd put on the full-length LP titled *Where Are You?* with "The Night We Called It a Day" and for me his still-compelling rendition of "I Cover the Waterfront." That album was quintessentially '50s—Frank's portrait on the cover rendered in pastel chalk, wearing a v-neck cashmere sweater, the ubiquitous cigarette and smoke part of the romantic, lonely atmosphere of that era.

What a world—going fast, but I had little idea. I never heard a note of Charlie Parker, Lester Young, John Coltrane, Johnny Hodges, Ben Webster, or Sonny Rollins; no Nancy Wilson or Dina Washington—in short, no one with a saxophone and no one black, no serious jazz until I was in my twenties. In my early teens, I enjoyed Motown, of course, the Supremes and girl groups like the Shirelles, the Ronettes, the Crystals, but mainly then I cared about surf music, twangy Fender Stratocaster instrumentals, and later the psychedelic electric montage. Rock music from the '60s and '70s needs little explanation other than to say it was tied tightly to the social fabric of the times—whatever changes were taking place—and a good deal of it I'm now musically embarrassed to admit I ever listened to.

Yet despite an early diet of Dion and the Belmonts, Rosie and the Originals, and the Top 40 blasting out of KACY in Ventura, KRLA in L.A., or over KIST in Santa Barbara, some relatively complex sounds eventually made their way through to me. In the late '70s, fresh out of graduate school and teaching part time at Fresno State University, I was introduced to Ben Webster by the poet Peter Everwine. Jon Veinberg, Chuck Hanzlicek, and some other local writers were getting together one evening at Peter's for a drink before dinner, and as soon as Jon and I stepped out of the car we could hear something amazing sliding up the walk toward us from Peter's open door. Webster's saxophone sent gravity waves out in the melody and hit you just below the solar plexus, moved you to a space you'd never been in before, slowed the rankle of the day down to nothing and almost let the music breathe for you. I could hear his horn breathing too, that after-flutter on the notes ending a phrase, some overheard angelic murmur. Webster simply had more volume than any other sound I had heard—not loud volume, but weight and space volume, the way a soul is full, I suppose. In Peter's living room we saw two speakers on stands as tall as we were, and then the stereo gear stacked up looking like the cockpit of a 747—gauges and dials, a turntable set on a slab of marble and that slab with some kind of rubber suction cups beneath it, anchored to another set of cups on the top of a tuner. There were no wires; there were cables—gold-filled, we were informed. Hearing Webster on all this apparatus, we agreed: gold-filled! This was sound that massaged your blood, that calmed your psyche. Coming down the walk into Peter's house, Jon said he didn't know who that was playing, but it made him want to get a bottle of good whiskey and drink it right on down. Webster had a searing intensity, huge tone, and distinctive timbre. He was blowing "Body and Soul" and we were sold. I went right out to some local record stores and bought every Ben Webster album I could find, a couple where he paired up with Coleman Hawkins, who was rougher, with more of an edge. But it was Ben Webster who had the sound, that signature flutter behind the notes. I bought *Soulville* and *For the Guv'nor*—his tribute to Ellington—and his album recorded in Copenhagen, *Saturday Night at the Montmartre*. He was featured on Ellington arrangements of "All Too Soon" and "Stardust," and backed up folks like Billy Holiday, Ella Fitzgerald, and Carmen McRae. Listening to an hour of ballads by Webster, his incomparable soothing and soulful way with a melody line, would, I swore, cure arthritis, depression—everything but a stack of compositions due back on Monday. Why hadn't I heard of him before this?

I moved from Fresno State to the University of California in my hometown, Santa Barbara, in the summer of 1980. One evening I went by my father's house and after dinner mentioned Ben Webster to him, but he had no reaction. He had just discovered a re-mixed early Artie Shaw album with a young Mel Torme singing. While I still liked the Glenn Miller or Tommy Dorsey he often played, and Artie Shaw was OK, I wondered how he had overlooked some of the most soulful and sophisticated music of his time, old recordings that many of us were trying hard to find in shops those days. Class probably came into it. Bars, jazz clubs, roadhouses—my father, as the expression has it, "did not much hold with drinking." A lower class of people frequented those places, listened to that music. He'd have a glass of his Mogan David concord wine or a sip of low-priced champagne once a week, but red wine was somehow beyond the moral scope of things—and then there was booze. He just felt above or apart from people who drank, and so their music also I guess, although he can't possibly ever have really listened to it. You don't have to be much of a deconstructionist to see the racial implications in all of that, but he never did. It was, for him, just a question of the music—that was the only criterion, as he saw it, and, as in everything else, he was sure he knew what was best.

He just couldn't acknowledge the ties to jazz, even though a favorite of his, June Christy, had a foot firmly in that camp. In the '40s and early '50s her husky, enticing sound and narrow vibrato delivered a sexy and stylish torch song without sacrificing a wholesome quality. "The Misty Miss Christy" replaced Anita O'Day in Stan Kenton's orchestra before going out on her own. She had early hits with "Tampico" and "How High the Moon," which was a tune that, even at five years old, I recognized on the radio. We always listened to my father's station while driving in the car, so if I could recognize her voice, that meant he played June Christy a lot. Around that time, she topped *Down Beat*'s poll four years in a row as best female vocalist. Then, in 1955, Christy cut her first solo album for Capitol, *Something Cool*, and in this one the jazz element was clear, as she combined with Maynard Ferguson, Laurindo Almeida, and Bud Shank. I think it was about then that my father stopped playing her records.

There was a good live music series in the early '80s at the County Bowl in Santa Barbara, and I caught Muddy Waters, Bonnie Raitt, Joni Mitchell—my folk and blues hangover from the '70s. But the concert I enjoyed most was the Pat Metheny group—Metheny a man who was a magician with a guitar. I should say with several guitars, for onstage that night there had to be at least fifteen guitars upright on stands, and he moved back and forth between them for different effects, and on different numbers, and the sounds that came out were incredibly varied, a number of them sounding almost like a clarinet tweaked with electricity. He was playing a number of the selections from his group's new album, *As Falls Wichita, So Falls Wichita Falls*, songs that had a driving, fused center and incorporated a number of sound devices, one of them the rhythmic thwack and muted whir of a helicopter's blade, used as background and counterpoint against slower or higher-pitched riffs. Ornette Coleman was a major influence on Metheny, and in the combinations and clusters of notes and counter melodies you could hear it. Those days, I listened to FM mostly, KJOY out of L.A., all-jazz radio. I'd picked up a new double album by Sonny Rollins that offered most of his early recordings, crisp light tunes like "The Trolley Song" as well as some more deepwater ballads. I liked Rollins's swirling phrases, his loops, dips, and extrapolations—his tone most vivid and clear when he reworked mainstream melodies. I had six or eight Ben Webster recordings, and all the new and rereleased jazz greats. And yet if I were in an elevator or a shop and some early Tommy Dorsey song came over the Muzak—something a young Frank Sinatra, Joe Stafford, and the Pied Pipers sang—the entire lyric would come to mind the moment I heard the first phrasing of the melody, as if from the car radio that had been on as far back as I could remember.

And my father still had all his Julie London albums—Julie London, who was backed up by one of the best jazz guitarists of all time, Barney Kessel. No one had his polished, smooth chord-melody approaches. Even in seventh grade, I knew Julie London, partly because my father played her on the hi-fi all the time and partly because of her sultry and voluptuous album covers. In the '50s a low-cut cocktail dress was a cultural icon, but as boys we knew little of culture. Yet that album cover of Julie London with her red hair and black dress revealing most of her bosom—a portrait against a light sea-green background—got our attention. "Cry Me a River" vaulted her to fame, on the popular stations and on jazz stations as well. That entire first album was just Barney Kessel, a bass, and her. The seamless chord progressions and notes muted and singled out were perfect backup for London's low, persuasive, plaintive stylings.

To this day, I can still recognize Kessel on a recording, a clean, effortless, and inventive style that explored the range of a chord, its connotations to melody. But even this tangential popular side of jazz was fading by the late '60s. Kessel played with Artie Shaw in 1946 and the Oscar Peterson Trio in 1952 and 1953, and he was featured on the hit single "Poinciana" on Ahmad Jamal's 1958 hit album *But Not for Me*. One afternoon I happened to turn to Steve Allen's talk show on the TV, and there was Kessel as part of the studio orchestra playing snippets of intro and commercial lead-ins, his genius lost among the thirty-second brassy upbeat bits of filler coming back from a station break. What a world.

Julie London married Jack Webb, who then was long past Sergeant Friday and was now a TV producer. They later divorced, and London married Webb's friend, Bobby Troop, of the Bobby Troop Trio, who wrote the theme song for the TV series *Route 66*. Nevertheless, they all remained friends and Webb starred her as a nurse in a black-and-white series called *Emergency*, a hit for a few years, in which he also cast Troop as an attending physician. Julie London was a good actress, and she made a movie or two in the early '60s, but she was no longer singing or recording. Whenever I came across *Emergency* as I was flipping channels, I always wondered why she had given it up. She still had the pipes, and there seemed to be a market for standards and torch songs, as they were then called, on some "easy listening" radio stations. Why wasn't she cutting a new LP of smoky ballads, singing somewhere in a supper club, for the twenty or thirty people who still knew what they were listening to?

WINGTIPS: SANTA BARBARA
AND STYLE IN THE '60S

Style, after all, is a kind of humor,
Something truly beneath contempt...

—LARRY LEVIS

"Hey, *ése*, your mama dresses you funny!" Fish Hernandez called across the school yard as my buddy Francis Orsua walked to his locker before first period at Bishop High. It wasn't Orsua's red letterman sweater buttoned only on the top button over his white T-shirt and dangling almost to his knees, nor the white Levis, which were worn tight and in the "high water" style a few inches above the ankles so his white sport socks showed. This was the regular gear. But beneath it all there was something flashy, a deep purple shine—it was the shoes.

1963, and clotheswise there wasn't much, so anything outside the standard issue got noticed. We were sophomores and wanted, as kids always have, to fit in, but compared to today, the pressure was minimal to nonexistent—no MTV, no cable, no advertising campaigns focused on teenagers. For good reason. We had very little money, as did most of our parents, and what we did have usually went toward repairing our rust-bucket Chevys, needed to get to school, to work, and up and down State Street on Saturday night, doing nothing but seeing and being seen.

What minimal style there was evolved from sources unknown. We did not have much by way of role models; there were not many tricks to pick up from teen movies. There were a couple of biker/Hell's Angels movies, and maybe one or two seniors wore black leather motorcycle jackets with the silver chains and zippers, wore them into the parking lot, then stuffed them in their lockers until school let out. Most of the time, though, when you saw teens and twenty-somethings in films they were dressed up like our parents in the '50s and early '60s—bad bland suits, and everyone "liked Ike." I still remember Sandra Dee in *A Summer Place* with her blond page-boy, a string of pearls around her neck, all the makeup, and stiff dresses. The same went for Natalie Wood in *Rebel Without a Cause*. And what about the "rebel" himself? As "far-out" as James Dean got in that film was a pair of blue jeans and a crisp red windbreaker; he had a haircut and I bet his shoes were shined. Sure, there were rock 'n' roll celebrities, but who was dressing them? Find a photo calendar of early Elvis and look at the stuff he was wearing; it was random and mis-matched and looked like it came from a Tupelo thrift shop. And who would want to claim to be behind Fats Domino's dark, tentlike suits? Besides, the emphasis was the hair—ducktails, flattops, big BIG jelly rolls—but that's another story.

Early '60s, the pickings were slim. Boys wore "white Levis," which were in fact beige, and which were made by Wrangler, Lee, and other makers as well. Any brand was acceptable, and we could wear them to school, whereas we could definitely not wear blue jeans (motorcycle-rebel-juvenile-delinquent gear). It would be years before jeans would lose their hoodlum connotation and Calvin Klein and company would make them into a fashion statement at five times the price. In 1963, you wore white socks, and loafers predominated, any kind of loafers, black, brown cordovan, penny or otherwise—they were "sharp," "sanitary"!

At our school, girls had uniform checked skirts, white blouses, brown uniform sweaters or blazers, and two or three acceptable styles of all-white or brown-and-white saddle shoes. Not much strain for wardrobe selection, for competition with others, or spending money on the latest thing. But they found it boring. The only variations were the skirt lengths, which were officially set at two inches below the knee but which some girls would adjust upwards by rolling the waist-bands once out of radar range of the nuns. Once a month, or even less frequently, the girls would have a "free dress" day and would arrive in everything from red formal dresses to regular skirts and blouses—no pants or shorts allowed.

I transferred to Bishop Garcia Diego High School, in my hometown of Santa Barbara, from Villanova Preparatory School, an hour away in Ojai. There, you wore suits each night to dinner and lined up alphabetically for inspection—shoes shined, tie straight, shirt clean. A few of us there wore white jeans, but it was nowhere near as universal as it was at Bishop. My first week there, I wore my white jeans and bought a new pair of black loafers at Rodenbecks and fit in. I was seen and not seen.

The '50s had not worn off, in mind-set or in fashion, if you could call it fashion. As exams came around, I was amazed to see the class presidents and officers showing up to school in suits and ties, as grey or brown and nondescript as their fathers' poplin suits from Penney's. For the students from relatively well-off families, a herringbone tweed jacket from The White House, maybe a camel-hair jacket by Hart, Schafner, and Marx from Silverwoods. The idea was that dressing up imparted a business or professional attitude toward the tests. I had just been freed from a restrictive environment (Villanova was known by one and all as the "Pink Prison") of suits, enforced study hall times, mandatory trips to the barber, et al., and was not about to get in line with that trend. Luckily, this Eisenhower/Dick Nixon/Robert Hall mentality seemed to dissipate over the summer. The next year we saw student leaders go off to conferences in suits, run for student office in suits, but that was about it. Few of us wanted to look like salesmen, the old fathers of the '50s.

For all of high school, low-cut, black Converse tennis shoes were popular. They were cheap and made for a quick transition from class to the basketball court. I never wore them, just didn't like how they looked—too much like the black tennies I wore as a kid. The other choice, after the loafer fad faded away, was deck shoes, a blue canvas, low-cut shoe that surfers wore. Sperry made the best shoe, with the thickest skid-resistant sole (originally made for yachters and sea-wet surfaces), arch supports, and sturdier blue canvas. Keds made a cheaper, thinner version of the blue deck shoe for about $9.00, whereas the Sperry's were $14.95. A not insignificant difference in 1964.

Because this was southern California, and because it was something new, the surf look came on fast. White jeans were still the thing, but it soon became standard issue to wear a wool Pendleton over your white T-shirt. These long-sleeve shirts had two chest pockets, and there were only a dozen different designs it seemed, and most of us had one or two and recognized which ones the others wore—blue with black weave, dark brown with gold, a tan with brown lines. There were other makes of Pendleton-like shirts, but we knew the real things, the heavy cloth and fine stitching, and you could always check for the blue and gold label. A real Pendleton was close to $15.00, pricey in those days, but most of us, especially those who were surfing, forked over the extra money and smugly congratulated ourselves in our conformity. This and the brand of a couple kinds of tennis shoes were as close as our generation ever came to $159.00 Nike Air Jordans. Recently, rummaging through a thrift shop thirty-five years after the fact, I found almost a dozen perfectly good Pendletons on the rack, long-abandoned there at $3.95.

I'd been surfing since I was thirteen and had no problem adapting to the surfer look, though I did find it amazing when, one weekend night, I went to the Santa Barbara high school auditorium for a screening of Bruce Brown's classic surf film, *Endless Summer,* and there were about four hundred of us all in white jeans, T-shirts and Pendletons, and blue deck shoes. Had we been ordered to dress that way by some authority, it never would have happened. As it was, we must have felt what any members of some large group feel when they are all together for the same reason, looking the same—safe, accepted, a self-congratulatory glow. What did we mean? What could you mean at fifteen or sixteen? It was social. It was unplanned peer pressure, but no one was killed for their shoes—almost everyone could afford the few modest choices of what then was seen as "boss."

On the outside we were all more or less proclaiming some fellowship of surfing, some shared social status or level or class. However, when you arrived at your favorite surf spot, you knew who were locals and which guys were from out of town. All you had then was your board—twenty-five different makes—and your surf trunks; most were nondescript, canvas or nylon, dark colors or bright patches, but no one really cared. There was a rage for a while for "rice paddies," trunks that looked like they were made from the 50- or 100-lb. burlap sacks that held rice—white or cream-colored with blue and red lettering and symbols. I had a pair and thought they were the best, wore them until they shredded from use and salt. I still have a mental picture of myself in my tan sixteen-year-old body, in my rice paddy trunks, slowly walking the nose of my board on a nice four-foot curl at Hope Ranch Beach. For that moment, in my very with-it surf trunks, in good position on a crisp wave, moving through the water and air, I was someone in the world, "stoked" and in style.

As my junior year started, there seemed little room to make a fashion statement; white jeans carried over with nothing new on the scene, which was diluted with vestigial loafers, the old, black low-cut Converses, some blue deck shoes, and as always the few nerds and math whizzes with their plain, brown, sensible leather shoes. Then Orsua showed up in his huge pair of Cordovan Florsheim Imperial Wingtips. Those shoes had to weigh ten pounds. As Fish razzed Orsua that morning from down by the vending machines, I immediately recognized what he was giving him gas about: my father—who was a real clotheshorse—bought his sport jackets and slacks at Silverwoods and Tweeds & Weeds, his shoes always Florsheim—had three or four pairs of them. These shoes had half-inch leather soles and almost inch-thick heels; they had a thin leather overlay with small holes punched out in a decorative pattern covering the toe and extending low along the sides, with a jagged top edge, a trailing ribbon of the design winding around to meet in back of the heel—the "wings" in wingtip. They laced up with those hard, thin, waxed, round laces; they clanked and clopped on walkways and asphalt—no one at school had them, and in every way they were "bad."

Orsua caddied at the Valley Club golf course in Montecito, for folks like Bing Crosby and others less famous but more wealthy. He saw his first pair there. A couple afternoons later, he tuned in the

Lloyd Thaxton dance show from L.A. on TV and saw the cutting-edge L.A. surfers wearing white jeans, shirts and ties, cardigan sweaters, and wingtips—doing the Surfer Stomp, the Bristol Stomp, the Locomotion, tossing great shaggy masses of blond hair about as their wingtips proclaimed their eminent, expensive weight across the floor. As soon as he'd saved up the $39.95 plus tax from his caddying job, Orsua went directly to Rodenbecks and told an astonished salesman that he wanted to try on a pair of wingtips, the Florsheim Imperials in cordovan, the top of the line. Before he turned to go to the back and check for his size, before he asked Francis to sit down, take off his shoes, and fit his foot into that silver measuring stick with the sliding bit on the side, he said, "You do know these are $39.95, right?" Francis was the first kid on his block, the only one at Bishop High, but not for long. They were three or four times as expensive as any other shoe. I was working at Jordano's grocery and could save up to buy a pair in three or four weeks, providing I cut back on most everything else. Eventually, I went to Silverwoods and bought a pair of cordovan Imperials just like Francis's from Sal Bonilla, the salesman my father always went to. We often wore them to school, not saving them for special occasions. We, in our crazy blood and impressionable heads, were the occasion.

Soon we bought a second pair. One of our group, Turbo Kuehl, had purchased some tan and calf-tone wingtips, and we backed up our cordovans with a pair of those—Florsheim and just as well made, but with not quite the heft and gloss of the Imperials. We eschewed the black wingtips, as they looked too much like priest shoes, and wingtips made by lesser brands often showed up in black. Our pals Steve and George sported some dark brown wingtips from Thom McCann, and although they were OK, they were not Florsheim Imperials. We wore them often, and we wore them down and had them resoled. They were clunky on our feet but we were going nowhere fast; we wanted to give the admiring public a chance to check them out. Extravagant as they were, they made a statement about quality, individual style; they peeled a layer off the standard of uniformity and were worth it. Wingtips raised us up in the world of our own imaginations; they improved the unimaginative world of the early '60s and gave us a good, groundless sense of our own importance. They had us feeling swell (as we soon stopped saying) as we floated down the sidewalks in the small, glittering bubble of air that surrounded us for that moment. *Retro.* Wearing such gleaming purple accoutrements for the feet—at once outrageous and old-school—elevated us in the air of our own estimations. We were retro decades before anyone would ever think to use the word.

Wingtips were our badges, our code, and the fact that next to no one cared didn't bother us a bit. However, as time went on, we made further moves in the direction of sartorial splendor. It was 1964 or 1965, and we were getting ready for one of the yearly big dances at school, probably the Mission Dance, which was held every year with a pageant, the meaning behind which none of us ever knew. What we did know was that for boys it meant dress shirts, thin ties, slacks and sport coats, shined shoes. It meant you saved up a couple weeks' wages to take your date out to dinner at the Harbor restaurant on Stern's Wharf, the Green Gables, or the Talk of the Town. The girls had their hair whipped, ratted, and twittered up into beehives and bouffants, had high-heeled shoes dyed to match their dresses, which were stiff and often sewn by their mothers. Some even wore white gloves—that long ago... For this dance, my girlfriend, Kathy Quigley, was going with someone else because her parents, as they often did, applied one of their rules about how many dates she could have with the same boy in a row. Orsua suggested I take Chris Espinosa, younger sister of our friend Billy, a girl who was a good dancer, and so I did. Francis, Billy, and I had actually been practicing a few new moves for the dances— variations on steps we'd made up, borrowed, or were common dance lingo then, such as the Slauson, with its kick and double clutch.

Months before the dance, we had decided to dress alike, establish some style. In truth, we were probably Dave Clark Five, or Gerry and the Pacemakers wannabes, before, of course, there was such a thing. We decided on the usual thin black ties worn with tab collars, red vests, blue blazers, and grey slacks with shoes we called "Italian fence climbers"—they were great for dancing, with thin soles, thin black leather, and half-inch-high bootlike heels and pointed toes. We were in the middle of the British rock 'n' roll invasion, and this was how the bands looked, and these especially were the shoes they wore. We looked pretty conservative, could have walked right into a Rotary Club meeting, except for the shoes, but they disappeared, of course, in the dark of the dance floor. The '60s were only radical at the very end, as they moved into the '70s. Check the photos and film clips of the Beatles' first landing in America for *The Ed Sullivan Show* in 1964, standing on the top of the ramp pushed up to the Pan Am jet—coats and skinny ties, pointy boots, and hair that, while very risky in length then, looks very moderate by any standard after that time. Orsua and I had been letting our hair grow, a bit over the collar, longer bangs—the basic Beatles' style, the one that prompted Father Bernard, the school disciplinarian, to tell us to see a barber or not to bother coming to school on Monday. Nothing more than fashion, and soon the fashion for hair would be very long. Father Bernard never commented on our wingtips.

This was for fun, all of it. We used to shine up our Imperials and walk downtown in the afternoons on weekends just to see how everyone looked. There were the usual suspects in jeans and Converse tennis shoes, the surfers, the rich kids out shopping with their parents, decked out in light blue oxford-cloth shirts and polished cotton slacks, wearing penny loafers the color of oxblood, a Montecito staple. But further down State Street the show improved. There were Southwick's and Dunnal's, where you could pick up work clothes and boots, army and navy surplus, and where a number of kids bought the fatigue jackets and Navy peacoats that were in for a while.

For the more classic Western and Mexican styles, there was El Patio Men's Wear. There was also always a small group or parade of "pachucos"—slick-dressing Mexican kids from the east side of town mostly, who went to Santa Barbara Public High School. For them, pomade was still very much in use, and hairstyles were pasted back with shine or large jelly-roll fronts. In those days pachucos wore chinos, a kind of polished cotton pant only a bit more baggy and sturdy than slacks, and friscos, a black, shiny jean that was worn with a cuff.

Often they wore those pants high waisted and had a beige or cream-yellow or white rayon shirt buttoned to the top button around the neck. Their standard coat was a cashmere suburban jacket that was half wool. For shoes, a high gloss spit-shined French toe was the thing, a square toe with one line of stitching across it, and usually in black. Everything shined, was slicked back and "spiffy"—this was for pride as well. This, for most of these kids, was all they had. Also up and down State Street were the car guys, who had a bit of a uniform but who almost didn't care—the cars were the thing for them. Usually car guys, like Joe Andrach or Chuy Blanco, just had blue jeans and white T-shirts, often rolled at the sleeves, and rough, black work boots, and sometimes an unbuttoned shiny, new, blue short-sleeved shirt over the T-shirt, especially if it was Saturday night cruising. Little differences, all affordable, a limited selection for each group with which to please themselves cruising in old cars or walking in style along the wide sidewalks of the past.

We didn't start a new fad with our wingtips; still, we wore them daily and on most occasions through to graduation in 1965. And I wore what was left of my wingtips to my first year in college. The cordovans had disintegrated by that point, having taken on numerous reheelings and resolings, but the calf-tones survived, and, in terms of practicality, I had one good pair of shoes to wear. It very soon didn't matter what you wore, as this was 1966 and 1967, and the real '60s were starting to kick in. I attended St. Mary's College in Moraga, just over the hill from Berkeley. All of our official dances were held in old hotels in San Francisco, and for them the usual gear was in order—shirt and tie, sport jacket and slacks. In four years, I noticed no real fashion statement beyond the blue work shirt and the psychedelic, tie-dyed T-shirts and glowing, flowing garments worn by the hippies, by Janis Joplin, Hendrix, Grace Slick, and the group. We weren't thinking much of clothes anymore. Orsua and our friend Steve Schiefen didn't have to think at all, as they had theirs issued by the Marines and the Army; they had one pair of boots, functional. What a luxury to worry about your clothes, how you looked, who you were likely to impress or not, when so many were worrying about living through another afternoon in Indochina.

I was too busy trying to figure out what I cared enough about to follow through with for the rest of my life. I knew that four years in college might well be it for fun, for freedom, for intellectual luxury; a life of work was staring me in the face right after that, or the draft. I think it was summer, home in Santa Barbara between my sophomore and junior years, working grocery again, when I realized my last pair of wingtips was done for, holes starting again in the soles, breaking down at the sides. I may also have realized that I was the only guy at the time still wearing them, and at some point, somewhere—at a dance, a kegger, or wedding—among people I knew or did not know, it must have registered that I looked a little ridiculous. After a summer of working, wearing out cheap shoes bought for the job, I had enough money to buy some decent new shoes for my next year in college, and, truth be told, I now have no idea what I bought or wore. I was pretty sure that Orsua had his Imperial wingtips finely polished and stored away in tissue paper and a box at his parents' home, saving them for his return from the war. If they still fit, he'd be plenty happy to wear them regardless of what anyone else was wearing or thinking then.

I remember taking my wingtips, along with a few other odds and ends from my aunt's house, down to the Salvation Army on lower State Street. In those days, no one but the truly needy shopped at a thrift store. Although they were worn, I hoped some poor soul might pass by the window and see them there, alongside some beaten brown and white spectators from the '40s perhaps, and recognize the wingtips' superior style and brand. I hoped they'd catch his eye, and he'd go in and run the sleeve of his raincoat across the toes until they almost shined, and wear them out into the world, his spirits lifted, and for a few minutes, feel like someone in the world.

MY LUCKY STARS:
COSMOLOGY, SCIENCE,
PHILOSOPHY, AND CARS

Luck. The luck to be alive. The luck to be anything—something, as Parmenides has it, instead of nothing. Given all the star dust in the universe—90 percent of it dark and unshining—what luck to end up anywhere, let alone in Santa Barbara by the glistening sea at the end of the '50s and in the early '60s; to be behind the wheel of a Chevy or sports car, blissful, unconscious, mentally glazed with the times; to not think of stars, really, as anything but distant and intangible light, romantic augmentation to the unaccountable continuum of your young life; to look up and see the artificial twinkling, the heavens in their plausible verisimilitude in the dark vault of the Fox Arlington Theater when you were seven; to roll down the window and look out to stars—sentimental emblems of themselves—as you parked the Bel Air on a cliff overlooking the beach; to have no idea which ones might be looking out for you in that most metaphorical of senses, which lucky clichés were glimmering up there, sustaining things behind the scenes, which angels were moving dust from one place to the next so you might slide by unscathed—to have, happily, no idea which stars to thank or blame…

I was coming up sideways, and fast, on the eight-foot-high cement wall surrounding the Clark Estate, and I wasn't feeling lucky—I wasn't feeling anything, numb in the instant with fear. I'd spun out my father's sports car, speeding on tires as slick as seals through the S turns along the bird refuge. I'd lost it and was twirling into the oncoming lanes, tires skating on the asphalt, then finally grabbing and sending me back where I came from, ready to smack that wall broadside, only inches away when everything stopped—as they said then, on a dime—as the torque bit and flung me back again across all four lanes of Cabrillo Boulevard, where, uncharacteristically, there was no traffic, where I kept going, smashing through a wooden guard post, its fifteen-foot length of chain that theoretically protected the pond shooting up into the air and coming down on the top of the car, abrading the cream-white paint job as I stood on the breaks, stopping two feet from the edge of the brink.

My pal O'Reilly had followed me. He pulled over, yelling for me to get out of the car, and then he jumped in and checked that it would start, put me back in the driver's seat, saying there was still no one coming either way and to get the hell out of there while he grabbed the post with my front right fender paint on it and threw it in the back seat of his old Oldsmobile. We beat it out of there up the roads into the hills of Montecito where I lived, stopping short of my drive to toss the wooden post down a steep embankment of wild ivy and plumbago.

I always thought I never had any luck—rarely got the girl or won the election, had parents who were rich, or got the cushy job—but in matters that really counted, and which I thought little about—life, for example—I did.

What else in the world could account for the lack of traffic either way on busy Cabrillo Boulevard, only minor dents to the car, stopping eight inches from the wall and flung across four lanes untouched—not a bump, not a bruise, 60 MPH when I lost it, a friend checking up on me, upset over a girl, completely sober, completely stupid, and going hell-bent for whatever, down the streets to take it out on what? I hadn't a clue—knew nothing beyond some teenage self-pity, rage, and despair of stars, nothing beyond that wall coming up fast.

And though a quick check with logic and the laws of motion said I was going to get smacked good and proper, I fully expected to still be there afterward, conscious and coming out the other side, though I could have just as easily been on my way back to molecules and possibly a truly unconscious state in which you do not have the luxury, the luck, to grow beyond it and look back, to finally realize what a frail boat the body is moving through the dark, directed by a boy of sixteen who, metaphors aside, was pretty much sleepwalking through his life.

Of course there are the physics, the math, every action with its equal and opposite reaction; someone could calculate the resistance and the force, the formulas of friction and mass, why and how spinning one way, I'd stop just short, then shoot back again the same way, not even a sore neck to show for it—and no one using seat belts in those days. Then again, who made up the physics and the rules? The closest I ever came to a Grand Unified Field Theory was Bible history and the Hebrews choosing Yahweh as the one god. For a long time, it would never get any more complicated than that. Now, of course, I know, know how lucky we are that the symmetries broke apart a few nanoseconds after the Big Bang, that gravity and magnetism and electricity and such were split up, that that asteroid hit in the Yucatán, killing off all the dinosaurs so the mammals could crawl out from under their rocks and be fruitful and multiply, so eventually we could walk around upright, wave our hands over our heads, and drive cars almost into walls—all this luck coming down to us, just waiting there, before we were cousins to protozoa or even began working our way up from fish.

Yet, now as then, it seems immensely improbable that I could manage that many out-of-control spins and have some equation of energy account for every one of my cells being in place when I finished. I forgot about it, of course, after a few days, after a few weekends of not being able to use the car, and did not even think about it enough to attribute my narrow escape to physics or to luck. Go figure.

I almost failed every science class I had to take, and about the gift of my life I took everything for granted—like gravity, like light, like the capillaries minutely connecting the arteries and veins, our bodies to the air, the fruit-ripe basket in which we carried forth our souls. Aristotle proclaimed there were nine windows of the soul, which seemed as good a number as any, as I don't think I took the opportunity to see out of any of them. I would go on, survive, get into college, study a little and pass my philosophy and other classes. By the time I was a senior, I would have had all I wanted of Plato and, being a closet poet then, would be a bit put off by being tossed out of the Republic despite how Greek and theoretical it was. Moreover, I would be truly exhausted with Aristotle's investigation into "treeness," or at least our instructors' attenuated questioning in his name for three out of the four years. As seniors, we compelled our new instructor—a young, part-time lecturer from Berkeley who had just received her MA—to let us read *Soul On Ice* and bring in bad poetry to class. This was 1968–69, and no one wanted to be someone who wasn't "with it," so we felt good about ditching Aristotle in favor of Eldridge Cleaver and Rod McKuen. I would not see my good luck then to have read philosophy, the luck that would leave me with something to mentally fall back on twenty or thirty years later when my sense of the liberal arts had grown beyond the Jefferson Airplane and the Rolling Stones and I wanted to examine cause or lack of cause in the universe, in its subatomic parts. By then, the nature of trees was a subject I had already learned in high school, literally backwards and forwards—I knew it cold, firsthand, driving into them. Otherwise, it was all molecules, atoms, and science. I knew a chair, I knew a tree—and I'd rather have run over the chair.

But that night I'd split up with my beautiful girlfriend, again. Everything I was sure I wanted—predictable Ozzie-and-Harriet life, kids, station wagon, meat loaf, stucco house, summer-weight sport coat and thin tie—washed out again. I wouldn't see my good luck with such romantic bad luck until I was almost thirty and onto myself enough to realize I'd never have lasted with all the dull and prescriptive happiness of suburbia—didn't really want it, wanted to go a whole different route than everything we grew up with. Lucky to have my heart broken, to escape with my life.

I never wondered, then, who was doing the programming. I never once thought about guardian angels, had not thought about them since I was seven and running around in short pants and white shirts in parochial school with stars pasted on my collar for my stellar pronunciation in French class. Now, there was all the glitter and Tabasco of the blood going crazy in my veins at seventeen. The subtext was elementary—I was going to live forever, car crashes notwithstanding. Each bright breath I took in each morning there by the sea told me this, and when I had close calls with the material world, the world of physics and car parts whizzing past my ears, the question of fate and the possibility of an ordered universe never registered. I was running free amidst the invisible confetti of chaos theory, and, unconscious or not, I was a long way from being through testing the schematics, seen or unseen.

I hadn't learned much—in physics class or about driving cars and paying attention in the world. My father had the roof and fender of his Porsche repaired, and after a couple months, I was again allowed to take it out Friday nights. My father hadn't learned much either. We were not rich, or even upper middle class; we were just average, with a house and mortgage, hi-fi, Pepsi-Cola and sandwich meat in the refrigerator. In 1963, a 356 Normal Porsche was only a little more expensive than a Chevrolet Impala. Besides, my father ran a radio station and simply traded out advertising time with the Volkswagen dealer down the street for the car. This, too, was lucky. Had he traded for a Volkswagen instead—one of those popular lightweight sardine cans—I might not be writing this. But he liked how the Porsche looked. He rarely changed the oil or bought new tires and lugged the engine driving in too high a gear. Consequently, I felt it my duty to put it through its paces at every available opportunity, which translated to any good curve or hairpin corner through Montecito or the Hope Ranch section of town. I knew this was a well-made automobile by how well it hugged the asphalt and allowed for a controlled four-wheel drift, but I didn't really know how reliably it was built until a few months later heading to a dance.

That night, I was over on the east side picking up my friend Orsua and his friend Desmond Olivera to go to the Earl Warren Show-grounds, no doubt to hear the Dartells again, the top local group in the tri-counties, play "The Dartell Stomp" or "Hot Pastrami"—hit songs with the usual wobbly organ and guitar instrumentals, simple beat, and two mumbled phrases that passed for lyrics. We each had on pressed white Levis and our eccentric cordovan wingtips, thinking we were someone all right in the world. Orsua lived on Indio Muerto Street, and pulling away from his house there was just enough road to get going before down-shifting for a big right curve at the end. A calm residential area, there was usually no traffic, and I could goose it through the turn and slip through where Voluntario crossed before shifting into third. Usually. It was an unmarked intersection—there were still such things—meaning no stop or yield signs either way. Olivera was hunched up in the tiny back seat, Orsua was riding shotgun, and two seconds after I roared moderately out of the turn and was in the middle of shifting, Orsua yelled "Look out!" as he saw the huge moon of a headlight aiming down on him. We were T-boned in the middle of the intersection by a '50s Merc loaded down with enough chrome and heavy metal panels to take on a tank. It hit square on Orsua's door, and then there was a dark second or two I lost forever between impact and when I remember the car landing kitty-corner across the intersection and plowing down the sidewalk. I hit a small pepper tree, overcorrected into a eugenia hedge, came back the other way, and bounced off a telephone pole before ending up cattywampus in some unfortunate family's front yard.

Dazed and confused didn't begin to describe it. The right side of the car was crushed, but Orsua was OK, as, somehow, was Olivera in the back. I pushed open the door and almost immediately two older—in their midtwenties—guys in black bowling shirts stuck their heads in and said, "*Futas*, you crazy kids give us the booze now before the cops come." We crawled out the driver's side as if stepping out of the spin cycle of a giant washing machine, patting ourselves down to make sure we were all there and in one piece—looking in the sideview mirror at our teeth—they were all there, and all our parts were straight, every Brylcreemed hair still in place. People were peeking out beneath their living room curtains, and a siren started up at the far end of Milpas Street. The windshield was cracked, split in a starburst pattern, the right fender was caved in, closed around the tire, a flat tire, the left front fender mangled as well, and, as we would later learn, the front axle was also broken. Orsua went back to the other car to check that the woman and the guy with her were OK. People gathered and we stood in the dark, our eyes wide in the glare of the cops' flashlights like fish caught above water.

For half an hour or more, we stood there feeling like refugees from our own lives, which we were. The odds, we never thought of

them. We should have been hamburger, bloody rags among the olean-
ders. When we talked about it a few days after, it was all attributed to
sturdy German engineering, a well-built solid construction had saved
our skins; having survived so well, it was only logical. Sure, I was lucky
that the insurance would cover most of it; lucky that Orsua lived close
to that intersection so I didn't have the time to build up any more
speed; lucky the woman driving the Merc was doing 50-plus MPH and
the police wanted to prosecute her instead of me; lucky I only received
a ticket for going 25 through an unmarked intersection whose
unposted limit is 15 MPH. But it didn't fully register.

What about those guys—where did they come from right after
the crash, asking about booze we didn't have? And who was that
pachuco in the silver sport coat leaning against the pole in the violet
light of the street lamp, cleaning his fingernails, waiting for someone,
nonchalant as metal met metal, and steam and oil ascended the air?
Who waved to me from across the street as we crawled out into the
night and then disappeared in the lights from the police cars once we
were all standing on the sidewalk, shrugging our shoulders, looking
up to the stars for answers?

We tried to respond, unable to explain anything beyond the vortex
of collision and the pinball effect of ten terror-bright seconds in the
dark. We didn't know much, but at least subliminally, in our bones, we
must have known we were luckier than we had a right to be. We were
shaken, but we shook it off. Orsua and Olivera eventually walked back to
Orsua's house, fired up his rust-bucket '51 Chevy, and drove to the dance
on sparks and promises. I was given a ride home from the cops, who
kept shaking their heads as if they couldn't quite believe it, as if we'd
stolen something big and gotten away with it—we had.

Half a year later, my father had figured enough out not to tempt
fate further, and he sold the Porsche and bought a Plymouth station
wagon. Little temptation there. But I had, with my mother's help (my
parents divorced when I was eleven) picked up a '59 Chevy Bel Air, a
boat of a car in bronze and cream with huge tail fins fanned out to the
sides. An automatic, heavy and slow, it rode low to the ground but was
equipped with a big V-8 that managed to give it some punch. It was

primarily intended as transportation to and from school, but it saw plenty of the beach and the three bowling alleys in town where, at the pool and billiard tables, I first began to hone some sense of aesthetics—the *ars gratia artis* of a fluid stroke and a reverse-angle bank shot—but also where I was lucky enough to win most of my games and keep myself in gas money. Once I was cleaned out in fifteen minutes playing nine-ball at the Fiesta Bowl, but I was philosophical about it and didn't do anything stupid, didn't peel out of the parking lot in a rage. Being flat-out embarrassed helped with the lesson in humility. But I'd been foolish and arrogant and I realized it; I'd played someone I didn't know, someone obviously from out of town, relying on an inflated sense of my own talent and the few shots I had seen him take. I was set up and, beyond the standard deception only skill was at play; no amount of luck would have changed the outcome. The big boys hadn't yet shown up for the evening, and this ringer was just killing time with me. I was out $7.50 plus table time by the time I knew what time it was. I called it off after the second rack, paid up, and got out with my shirt. Why this line of reasoning didn't occur to me with cars, I have no idea.

I drove home over the back foothill roads, across snaky Stanwood Drive, which was replete with quick twists and sharp turns, the perfect road for a Porsche. Again, sober as a scientist, I was cruising home alone one evening and misjudged the condition of my retread tires or the proper entry to the hairpin I'd taken dozens of times, and, also misjudging my speed, I fishtailed midway in the turn. My tail fin whacked a great slice out of a sycamore, and that had me overcorrecting the slide and off the road through the brush, heading downhill toward the edge of an arroyo. I stomped on the brakes, but it didn't have the desired effect, and I was gripping for impact when the car yanked to a halt like a steer roped in rodeo—the front axle had snagged an oak sapling, and it wound around it enough to pull the car up short, with just the big chrome bumper in the air over the arroyo, one hubcap spinning off into the gully like a satellite or lost planet.

I walked up the road and found a house from where I called my resourceful car-guy friend Joe Bolduc for help; good thing he was home working on his Mini Cooper as my next option was a gas station tow truck I didn't have the money for. He showed up quickly in his parents' '58 Plymouth sedan with a chain, which he anchored to the Plymouth's frame before scampering down the hill to hook the other end around the back axle of my Chevy. He jumped in his car, dropped it into low, and proceeded to burn what rubber there was on those tires trying to buck that lead-sled of mine back up onto the road. No dice. Smoke from the tires plumed into the air as he left off the accelerator and slammed it down again. Then, just for a second, in between attempts, I swore I heard a bar of "Catch a Falling Star"— "Put it in your pocket, never let it fade away"—and in the smoke near the back of Joe's car, I thought I made out someone, someone smiling like Perry Como in one of those Kraft commercials on TV. Maybe Joe had left the radio on to one of his parent's stations, maybe I was dizzy with the toxic smoke from the tires and exhaust, dizzy with chrome and starlight?

But I put it quickly out of my mind as on the umpteenth try I heard a sound like a green branch breaking or another weight being dropped on the metal plate of an old-fashioned scales. My car broke free, and Joe managed to drag it back-asswards up onto the road. Amazing that it worked, that the sapling that had caught and saved me now released and saved me again, amazing that no one came along there for twenty minutes or more.

I was too much an adolescent to believe in guardian angels, in anything really. Having survived many years of Catholic school, I surely didn't want to subscribe to an ordered universe, cosmic personal entitlements, a kind of bank account you could draw on to varying degrees, everyone with a different balance to begin, for no reason anyone could ever tell you. But it didn't take too much philosophy or rocket science to realize I had to be close to overdrawn somewhere. The mathematical probability of stacking up a car three times and walking away with nothing but lost breath was not good. Were there cosmic debit slips, could your number really ever be "up," was the universe personal—it would be years until I wrestled with this and forty variations of fate, the fact that the Chinese have been saying for centuries there are no accidents. I was seventeen, I was close to paradise on the California coast. At worst, these things left you wondering, whistling when you looked back. I had just lucked out, as we said then, end of story. I shrugged and figured there was still plenty of time to make sense of my life.

The car started, I owed Joe one I probably never repaid him—lucky to have friends, lucky there was an oak sapling right there in the middle of nowhere before the arroyo, lucky I was able to stand there in the dark and smoke a Tareyton with Joe as we checked out his back tires, one burned down almost to the canvas. I looked up into the clear, oil-blue sky and sent my thanks in the general direction of the networks of light above me. I knew I wasn't going to hear bodiless voices sing above in Latin or a code from the distant spheres, and I felt pretty sure I wasn't going to see some chariot charge across the sky trailing an alphabet of flame—words of revelation or even warning for my unconscious conduct and the weak vessel of my blood. But I had a vague, but inescapable feeling that something had been looking out for me—angels, astrology, a few propitiously blessed bits of particle physics, unadulterated good fortune in the face of catastrophe. You name it.

I gave Joe nine bucks for a new retread, but before he drove off he contributed his take on the situation at hand—a bit exasperated after a half hour's hard work—telling me what a "close shave" this was, how I was cutting things a bit thin in the crash department. Was I stupid or what? Did I think I was some kind of lucky, indestructible sob, racing that pig of a car around these tight curves? Didn't I know anything?

"SLEEP WALK"

"If you remember the '60s, you weren't there" is a line often attributed to Dennis Hopper. But some of us managed to retain a few more grey cells than others, and Hopper is likely referring to the last few years of the decade and the wilder "Easy Rider" days. From ground level in the first half of the decade, it was certainly not all "the '60s," i.e., peace/love/tie-dye/Tabasco sauce/Hare Krishna/flower power/HaightAshbury/LSD/LBJ/purple haze/and Get Out of Vietnam Now!!! Most all of the above found fertile ground in the late '60s and early '70s, and their influence soon became acceptable, even fashionable, with long hair for TV network news anchors and baseball players, with most of the public in bell-bottoms and other gear, the stuff that made us look like we were working on the Pirates of the Caribbean ride at Disneyland.

The first half of the '60s was still the '50s—the same fashions (or lack thereof), music, and politics hung on. We were sleepwalking through our lives, repeating, like dreamers talking in their sleep, the taglines of our parents' Junior-Chamber-of-Commerce conservative certainty. And, arguably, the '50s were a continuation of the '40s: in 1943 the House Un-American Activities Committee banned Woodie Guthrie from the radio, citing his "communist sympathies." Well into the '60s, my father still thought McCarthy a hero and had no idea—few did then—that J. Edgar Hoover was wearing women's dresses.

We were simply blissful driving our rust-bucket Chevys to school and summer dances, burning up gas at 35¢ a gallon, and repeating the boilerplate social and political platitudes of the merchant class when the subjects came up, which wasn't often. We were listening to Elvis and the Everly Brothers, of course, but also to Sam Cooke's "You Send Me" and Fats Domino's "Before I Grow Too Old to Dream"—good tunes, albeit with lyrics as standard as those of any '40s or '50s ballad. What we really wanted was the sweet loneliness of the Fleetwoods' "Mr. Blue" or Roy Orbison's "Only the Lonely," but we were content with Marty Robbins's ballads such as "A White Sport Coat" and "El Paso." More to the point, no one switched the station when Percy Faith and his stringy orchestra came on with "Theme from 'A Summer Place'" or Ferrante & Teicher with their lumbering double-piano version of the theme from *Exodus*. How to account for that incongruous blend of "taste"—the middle-brow orchestral music of our parents infiltrating our Top 40 stations? We couldn't have been paying that much attention as the dull waves of one decade overlapped the next and lulled us half to sleep.

Sixth grade—1958—and we were living with transistor radios tuned into KACY from Ventura, KRLA in Los Angeles, and the "Mighty 690" booming up from just south of San Diego in Rosarito, Mexico. Barely teenagers, but we knew what we wanted—and it was as many drained and elongated rock 'n' roll electric guitar tracks as we could get. Duane Eddy, Jorgen Ingmann, the Ventures, and even an amplified and twanged-up instrumental version of an old western song, "Ghost Riders in the Sky," by a one-hit band whose name is as lost to me now as the 45 records (more than two hundred of them) I spent most of my allowance on all those years ago.

But that summer, 1959, the most popular and memorable guitar recording of the era was released, Santo & Johnny's "Sleep Walk." It hit Number One on the Billboard charts in September—an instrumental with only bass and reverberating slide steel guitars, and we went crazy for it. I loved the torpid bass and yawning guitar lead, those haunting whole-note bends pulled blind high. Man, that was the stuff! It would be Santo & Johnny's only real hit, and the rumor was that they recorded it in their living room, but who cared? It turned out that these two brothers from Brooklyn released at least two more singles, "Tear Drop" (which, like "Sleep Walk," they wrote) and then their version of the familiar big-band number "Caravan." The older brother,

Santo, played the steel guitar, and Johnny added in bass or rhythm. They also recorded two albums, but most of the songs were old standards and aimed at our parent's generation—"The Breeze and I," "Deep Purple," "Old Man River," "Prisoner of Love." In those years, though, all we ever knew about was "Sleep Walk," and it looked to us like Santo & Johnny were one-hit wonders too—but what a hit! Unlike most of the Top 40, "Sleep Walk" had staying power. All through the early '60s it was played at sock-hops, on hi-fis at parties, with live bands echoing that drawn-out melody near the end of school dances in the gym, and of course always on the rock stations as a "blast from the past." "Sleep Walk" translated and transported a good deal of our locked-down and inarticulate teenage emotions, and its slow, somnambulant rhythm let most everyone out on the floor in the warm, spinning dark before the dance closed down.

As we walked out of the Bishop Garcia Diego gymnasium in our purple robes at high school graduation in 1965, we had little idea about what was coming, good or bad. The Kennedy assassination, subconsciously at least, hadn't tracked with most of us; there was a skip in the record, and the same incredible notes kept repeating as we were continually assured by the old men in bad suits and black gowns that everything was correct and true. If anyone mentioned conspiracy, a whitewash by the Warren Commission, they were ridiculed. Arlen Specter, the commission's chief counsel, from Pennsylvania, dreamed up the "magic bullet" theory, a preposterous explanation that had a single slug breaking apart at eight angles to defy most of the laws of physics, thereby "proving" that Oswald had acted alone. The political powers saw Specter as a clear thinker—Specter who became a Republican senator and remains one today. Representative Gerald Ford would agree, actually changing the commission's report to read (wrongly) that the bullet wound was at the base of Kennedy's neck, which it would more or less have needed to be for Specter's hypothesis to be correct. That is, he falsified the evidence and went on to become vice president and later on president, moving through the usually contentious gauntlet of politics as if he were holding a complementary pass. He was. We couldn't see what was in front of us. On

older and seemingly sophisticated teens smile and do the latest dances, or hermetically seal themselves together in true-love embraces during a rare slow song. We wanted to see the Everly Brothers lip-synch their new release, "Dream," and Bobby Rydell, with his three-inch-high pompadour, do the twist while mouthing "Wild One." I loved Little Anthony and the Imperials, and the Shirelles, the Chiffons, and the segment when, after a brand-new song was played, Clark picked kids out of the crowd to appraise its chances of becoming a hit. "I give it an 86—I liked the beat and it's easy to dance to." What else then was there?

Rock 'n' roll fame had even briefly touched our town. A friend of mine, who then attended Goleta Union School north of Santa Barbara, was invited along with other sixth graders up to the KEYT-TV studio, a large pale building on top of the mesa between the town and the ocean, which you couldn't miss as there was very little else up there then. The girls were told to wear skirts or dresses—no pants or pedal pushers—and each had a dance card, filled in so no one would be left standing around alone at the edges of the floor like so many at regular school dances. No, they were invited to a special West Coast production of *Bandstand*, the granddaddy of all dance shows come all the way from Philadelphia with Dick Clark himself. A local DJ friend of my father's, Lou Stumpo, had started a teen dance party show, *Pacific Bandstand*, about this time for KEYT, the ABC affiliate in town, and a visit by Dick Clark's crew would be a big boost to local ratings.

Late '50s, early '60s: we were ready for the glitz and limited glitter of a rock 'n' roll dance party; what we were not ready for was the drudgery and formality of the mandatory dance classes offered by the nuns. Dick Clark had a dress code, to be sure—no one in blue jeans, capris, or black leather motorcycle jackets. The kids from Philly were neat, as far as America knew. But for us it was much worse. Girls wore stiff dresses, corsages at the waste, white gloves—a thick application of grace that was a throwback to the cotillion. Boys showed up in bland business suits and their father's old ties, sporting our first small constellations of safety-razor nicks. When we finally graduated from eighth grade, we were happy when the official ceremonies were over and kids had parties at their homes where we could at least play our own records. While parents kept a watchful eye from the dark corners, one or two couples danced as close as they then dared, to the envy of everyone else.

But I didn't learn quickly—not dancing, not what it could lead to. All that practice at school, moving our feet as if we were shuffling around the edges of a grocery bag placed on the floor, only led to Virginia Cortez and early heartbreak as she put her head on my shoulder and shorted out the entire network of circuits in my skin. The kids from our class at Mt. Carmel were at a party at Virginia's house after "graduation." The unknown and scary world of high school was out there, waiting for us—Santa Barbara Public High School, Bishop Garcia Diego High, or Villanova Prep over an hour away in the mountains in Ojai. But first the dance parties. At Virginia's, there were also kids from the crosstown school, Dolores, who would be going to the public high school in the fall, a place that seemed a lot more exciting and glamorous than the Catholic school. Lynne Ann Orlando and Greg Saleni were there as a couple, and Saleni had a reputation as a real tough, a fighter, a kid who worked at looking mean, insolent, raising his eyebrows and sneering with his wide lips at anyone who looked at Lynne Ann. No one looked. At twelve or thirteen, everyone was the same size, and all it took was a willingness to fight and a little aggression to get your way. In slightly over a year, though, everyone else would grow, and Saleni would turn out to be a small kid, a punk no longer a threat to anyone. For the moment, however, he decided to dance with Virginia while Lynne Ann talked with some girls. Virginia's dark eyes sparkled, and they danced again. What was I going to say? That I thought she liked me? I could feel that mollifying eighth-grade vision of romance slipping away. I hung out at the punch bowl in my blue oxford-cloth shirt and black lamb's-wool cardigan I'd borrowed from my father, looking as if I were there for an informal golf club meeting. I think Saleni actually had on a black leather jacket.

Bishop High was a small coed school, and you knew most everyone in your class. There were lots of dances, noon sock-hops in the gym (a holdover from the '50s), dances after football and basketball games, and about every other month an official dress-up dance for which the girls tortured their hair up into bouffants with lacquered waves of spray and made new dresses with high heels dyed to match. Bishop was not as academically rigorous as Villanova, and I wasn't worrying about grades or classes or going to college, and, as a sophomore transfer in 1963, I certainly hadn't given the least thought to visiting Indochina. I was thinking about dancing, as it became clear that to have a chance with girls you needed to dance. In my junior and senior years, Orsua, Espinosa, and I used to work out some new steps before each dance—a few crossover steps we'd made up, a kind of sideways back-kicking step, and a double clutch for the Slauson, a line dance before the cowboys were doing it. Given our goals of romance, of shining in the light like the kids on *Bandstand*, we didn't feel the least bit silly pulling out a portable hi-fi at someone's house and going over dance moves. Other than the dances, you had few chances to be close, to get to know a girl, especially if you didn't have a car. But regardless of your transportation, you had to meet someone first, and the dance was the place. Most of us were just trying to harness the hormones running like hard freight through our veins, to connect with one or the other objects of our wide-ranging affections.

I knew surf music and Motown, but even if I worked up the courage to ask someone to dance, I did not then know the spins, dips, and twists kids were pulling off with the Hully Gully, the Stomp, and the Mash Potato, gyrations that looked like varieties of religious experience. It was a record hop, and after a while someone put on some doo-wop, the Flamingos' "I Only Have Eyes for You," and the dancers froze, feet moving as if through a dance floor of fudge. I'd been watching a couple in the middle all night—the girl, a pageboy blond, all curves in a cotton dress and a tall guy who must have been on the basketball team—seniors who'd been melting into each other dance after dance, enough steam rising there to press a dozen shirts. Both her arms hung on his neck, his arms wound around her waist, as hot as it then got before you were thrown out and called into the office on Monday. Later, I'd learn how to duck out via the restrooms and meet girls at your car in the parking lot, how to keep an eye open while making out, to duck beneath the dash from the flashlight and the padre on patrol. For now, I thought how wonderful it would be to be that guy in the middle of the dance floor, all confidence and careless in love. The cliché about being careful what you wish for as you might just get it was something I wouldn't hear for many years.

Two and a half years later turned me loose in that exact spot, arms around Kathy Quigley, eyes closed as the Righteous Brothers' "You've Lost That Lovin' Feeling" ground any pretense of movement to a halt on the floor. It was getting toward the end of the dance, and "Sleep Walk" came on next, with its bone-deep bass laying down a line of hormones like a fever in the blood—the high, sliding lead stringing-out a last legitimate embrace, seeming to lift all the sighing dreamers out of the transoms of the gym into the starlight, spinning through the blue spring night. Last dance of the year, time to walk out those double metal gym doors, rubbing our eyes, dizzy with our own entranced blood buzzing in the dark. We had to kiss quickly so that she could get home by midnight—some part of the world still that careful and slow.

We had only a few dates that summer as Kathy's parents were pressuring her to date other boys and I was going away to college, while she had one more year of high school remaining. After the last time I took her home, I drove around our then still reasonably sized town. I pulled into Peterson's Drive-In on upper State Street at 1:00 A.M. for a vanilla milk shake, which I drank in the car as I drove, going nowhere with the windows down, with that twang and groundswell bass from Santo & Johnny still pulsing in my head, sure everything I wanted was right there despite college coming, and the war, the whole social and political catastrophe. I looked up into the night, where the stars slurred like the notes in the song, and eventually drove home like no more than a sleepwalker gliding unconsciously through blue-deep air back to his bed.

After 1965 it was time to wake up. Bob Dylan, the Rolling Stones, and the Monterey Pop Festival, and the lyrics would be about politics and social justice instead of romance—even the Beatles were turning psychedelic. Jimi Hendrix set his guitar on fire on the stage in Monterey and wanted to know if we were experienced. We weren't. My father went on complaining about the liberals at UC Santa Barbara, wondering how many Communists were members of the Center for the Study of Democratic Institutions, and warning that the Reds would soon be coming across the border from Mexico to get us. For years he'd been saying we were moving to Spain. He admired Franco, who oversaw an "ordered" country, two Guardia Civil armed with machine guns on every other street corner. He kept telling me I needn't bother applying for college in the States: I would attend the University of Madrid. He talked for years, as if he had researched and arranged things, as if he would step off the boat or plane in Spain and everyone would speak English (he had not one word of Spanish), as if it were all set. In reality, I think maybe he'd picked up one travel brochure. Luckily, I'd started taking a great deal of what he said with a pillar of salt, and so even though Orsua and I almost missed the start of the test, having stayed out late after a dance, we took the college SAT. Orsua, who no doubt did better on the test than I did, would end up in the Marines, diving for cover when the missiles came into the flight line somewhere near Chu Lai. The test was three parts math and two English, and I ended up with a 799, a score good enough to keep me working at the grocery store. But some friends from Villanova were applying to St. Mary's College near Berkeley and so I had my test score sent there, as the Educational Testing Service reported one score for free, and at some point I must have mailed in an application. I was in luck. That year, St. Mary's standard for accepting young men into the freshman class was based on the ability to pay tuition, the ability to pay room and board, and the ability to breathe—in that order. Bless their financial disposition; without it, I would not have been admitted to college and would have found myself running through the jungles of Indochina or lining up for work at the sawmills in Canada, a choice I instead managed to postpone for five years.

By the beginning of my sophomore year at St. Mary's just over half of our freshman class had flunked out. Kathy was dating my trusted dance buddy, Espinosa. The war was here, student deferments were being cancelled, there were military recruiters stationed at tables in the halls of our classrooms, there would be a lottery for our lives. Nationwide there were protests and riots on moral, constitutional, and civil rights grounds. They would assassinate both Martin Luther King and Bobby Kennedy. As a nation we would again be given the "lone gunman" lie, which we would accept like someone under hypnosis, or someone sleepwalking through his own house, changing directions every time he banged a shin against a coffee table or chair. What, some of us asked ourselves, would ever be the same? Well, LBJ would quit and we'd get Nixon, along with Spiro Agnew and the deaths at Kent State. Politics as usual. Dick Clark's *American Bandstand*, with various permutations of stage sets and lights, clothes and hair lengths, would remain on TV through 1989, running thirty-seven consecutive years, including reruns. It had outlasted its competitors *Hullabaloo* and *Shindig*, both of which quit in 1966.

By that point events had shaken me awake. I still heard "Sleep Walk," however, at many different times and in all sorts of places, and it would always stop me for a minute or two. It was played at the "mixers" I attended early on in college, and it was a perennial favorite on "golden oldies" stations. Groups borrowed from it even into the '90s, such as the Cowboy Junkies, on their *Trinity* album, with their wonderful interpretation of "Blue Moon" and a bass line that owed everything to "Sleep Walk." Even now, it continues to come up in films, especially those set in the past. In *Eddie and the Cruisers*, a sleeper from 1983 featuring a very young Tom Berenger and Ellen Barkin, "Sleep Walk" plays in the background, the true poster song for the era, representing rock 'n' roll for the late '50s and early '60s, as Eddie and his band pull up for a gig in their '57 Chevy two-tone convertible. It's also heard in the background of *Mermaids*, with Cher and Bob Hoskins. In the sci-fi film *Twelve Monkeys*, with Bruce Willis, Brad Pitt, and Madeleine Stowe, "Sleep Walk" makes an appearance three times—twice as a background for a real estate ad selling the Florida Keys, which pops up each time Bruce Willis's character, James Cole, time-travels into the past. It's heard the final time he is pulled back into his present—our future—to be examined by the scientists. Cole has successfully tracked the virus that has devastated the earth, killing plants and animals and driving the surviving humans underground. To reward him, the scientists have placed, for his viewing pleasure, a large painting by the luminist Albert Bierstadt—the *Valley of Yosemite*—above the chair he is strapped into. It is an idyllic sunset in the Yosemite Valley, a few deer in the lower right, Edenic nature before the turn of the century. "Sleep Walk" plays as soon as the painting comes into view and is a perfect coefficient for that dream light coming out of the past.

More recently, in *Hearts of Atlantis*, starring Anthony Hopkins, "Sleep Walk" offers a respite from the scenes in which the "low men," the J. Edgar Hoover operatives, are after Hopkins's character. The few times when Hopkins and the landlord's son find a peaceful minute or so, without having to worry who might be watching from the street, "Sleep Walk" plays in the background. I continue to hear it in elevators, over the Muzak at the airport, and it gets played regularly on the old-fashioned jukebox in my favorite fish restaurant on the Santa Barbara breakwater. Only yesterday, in a place as removed and unremarkable as Pismo Beach, I heard "Sleep Walk" lilting out of the Splash, a fast-food and clam chowder spot on the small main street. The following day, in a thrift shop in Santa Maria, my wife heard it again, drifting over all the used dresses and suits. In the mid '90s, "Sleep Walk" was used as the background track in a Mazda commercial—a kid on a '50s-style bicycle riding past the glass front of a showroom full of shiny red sports cars, the announcer asking you to remember how, growing up, you always dreamt of that special car. The music comes up, inviting you to drift back into your dreams.

"Sleep Walk" truly was the anthem of our adolescence, of the end of an age, and not just our little part in it, but of a national mind-set that simply accepted the ways of the past and deferred to authority—a habit of thought that saw most everything in a reductive, silver-edged black and white that kept life, for many, comfortable. As myopic as we were, many of us eventually did grow up: when it was time, we allowed ourselves to become engaged. All the same, "Sleep Walk" is perhaps an emblem of some part of us we should not let completely go, a part of our lives too unconsciously sweet to last.

THE FIRST POET

I barely knew William Stafford. Over twenty-five years we spoke twice, exchanged three short letters. He was never my teacher, yet I learned a great deal from him. He was a presence every time I wrote a decent poem—a light, the kind of influence you don't even know is there until one day, many years later, you take stock and shake your head in amazement, and loss.

William Stafford was the first poet I ever heard read. Nineteen, and what did I know? Not much, though I thought otherwise. I did know I didn't know math. I had just flunked accounting. Fall semester as a sophomore at St. Mary's College completed, and I'd received my first-ever F. I'd also taken a C in economics, my only A coming in World Classics, a humanities reading and writing seminar. I didn't need an accounting course to know two and a half more years and I'd be booted into the job market, so I decided to enjoy what time and relative freedom I had left. I went to the dean of studies and changed my major from business to English. Brother Cassian asked what my father—who paid the bills and insisted my major be business—would say, and I replied that I would tell him later, which I did, right after he told me that he could no longer pay for my education. Good thing I switched, I thought.

Like many bleary-minded nineteen year olds in the '60s, I thought I knew poetry. After all, hadn't I been writing the stuff for years? Didn't I own several Moody Blues, Doors, and Richie Havens albums? Besides, I'd just become an English major and was taking Major British Writers with Mr. Townsend, the head of the department, a serious and exacting man. Up to that point, T. S. Eliot was the most

"contemporary" poet I'd read; I loved *Prufrock* and *The Wasteland*—
the imagery, high voice, and compelling music. But I hadn't the least
access to, or understanding of, the conceptual grids and allusions
behind it all. My interpretations turned out to be just that, my interpretations—miles off course. The class was full of juniors who
seemed to know every difficult and hidden thing in the text. I was
receiving a gentleman's C on my exams and papers, which meant I
showed up and completed assignments but was essentially clueless.

Yet I felt I knew poetry, and symbols. My own poems were elabo-
rately layered with them, recondite as rocks from another universe,
but I knew the code. My poor roommates. Business and political science majors, they had a hard time escaping my recitations. I'd position myself in the doorway and read a new one before they knew what
hit them. Who knew to whom I was speaking in my inflated junior-
league Eliot voice? My friends just wished it wasn't them.

I was thick enough then that none of this reaction to my aspirations deterred me from poetry. I was brooding and serious. I did not
wear a cape, carry a stuffed raven, or write with a quill by candlelight,
but I'm sure I postured as much as any aspiring poet. So there I was at
the end of a week's classes on Eliot and the "dissociation of sensibil-
ity," thinking I knew what was what about poetry and the proper atti-
tudes to assume to signal potential greatness.

Before we were dismissed from class that Thursday, Mr. Townsend
announced that there would be a poetry reading by William Stafford
the following Tuesday; we were quietly encouraged to attend. I didn't
know Stafford from Sappho, but I was going to go. Somehow, I got two
of my roommates to attend with me. Probably after a year and a half of
putting up with my "verses," they wanted to see if there was any hope
left in the world for poetry. Whatever the reason, all three of us turned
up at 1:45 in the little lecture room that adjoined the student union.

As a crowd of about forty filed in, Mr. Townsend, obviously
pleased to see us there, called me over with a couple other members of
our class and encouraged us to ask questions after the reading. After
we sat down, I saw Townsend talking to Stafford, a remarkably
unflamboyant and fatherly looking man, and I asked myself, could

this really be a poet? Weren't poets wild men in tie-dyed shirts, with electric hair? Brooding men with crow-dark eyes who wore old trench coats, who were troubled, their melancholy clear as a crown of thorns? Leonard Cohen—now he was a poet, right? This was early 1967, and Stafford read from *The Rescued Year*. The poems were altogether different from what I had expected. I was stunned. He spoke directly, in a calm and honest human voice. He had not written poems embedded with allusions and symbolism from a poetry-culture machine cranked up to ten. To be sure there was lyricism, compression, and inventive phrasing, but something was wrong—I was understanding this, so were my friends?

He read "Letter from Oregon," which begins with a direct address to his mother. You could do that? He read a poem about his father's death that presented a clear, secular, and scary fatalism. And then a long one entitled "The Move to California"—an environmental poem before anyone thought to write one. I'm sure we weren't thinking of it that way that day, but we picked up on the elements of nature, the poet naming them and offering them simple praise:

> Gasoline makes game scarce.
> In Elko, Nevada, I remember a stuffed wildcat
> someone had shot on Bing Crosby's ranch.

And we began to understand about our own effect on the land, especially when he concluded the poem with:

> It takes a lot of miles to equal one wildcat
> today. We moved into a housing tract.
> Every dodging animal carries my hope in Nevada.
> It has been a long day, Bing.
> Wherever I go is your ranch.

Yet for me, it was as much how he said it as what he had to say; he'd actually mentioned Bing Crosby in a poem—could this be high art? Would Mr. Townsend approve?

The poem that William Stafford read that day that stayed with me more than any other, a poem I show to my students still today, was "Fifteen," about a boy discovering a motorcycle by a bridge, on its side, its motor running. I knew about motorcycles. I did not know you could actually put yourself in your own poem, that you could be the speaker. Among other things, "Fifteen" is an initiation poem. One of its marvels is how well and subtly the poet turns or translates the experience, charges it with sexual nuance. The connections between the cycle and a woman are intentional. "I admired all that pulsing gleam, the / shiny flanks, the demure headlights / fringed where it lay." For a moment, the speaker is also charged with that energy, that access to a new world; he guides the bike to the road and, for the first time, looks forward in his life to the undiscovered territory of the body:

> We could find the end of a road, meet
> the sky on out Seventeenth. I thought about
> hills, and patting the handle got back a
> confident opinion. On the bridge we indulged
> a forward feeling, a tremble. I was fifteen.

And that of course was the problem: fifteen. Slightly too young (in those comparatively innocent days), almost there, not completely in charge of time and circumstance. The boy thinks to look for the rider, finds him just coming to, and turns the bike back over to him. No matter, it's a start, a taste of experience, a first step. The poem transfixes that exact moment when life first presents itself to you in a tangible array of possibilities, where you first have a hint of what might be out there, and, teetering on a threshold, know that living electricity and movement as part of yourself. You take it and shape it in your hands, if only for that moment. You don't get exactly what you were after, but you know it's you standing there, and you know a little more fully the world before you.

I was knocked out. I had no idea poetry could be like this, pure, personal, and resonant as anything I'd ever heard. After the reading Townsend called us over to talk with the poet. I wouldn't have thought this was the kind of poetry Townsend approved of, but a couple years later I would realize that one thing both men shared—and which Stafford had addressed in at least one poem—was that they had both been conscientious objectors during World War II. While the smarter students hesitated, formulating something intelligent to ask, I blurted out what was really burning in my brain: "Do you think it's all right to use 'I' in a poem?" I was receiving a classical education and had not even been exposed to William Carlos Williams. I'd obviously been over Elio-tized, especially there in the gathering social turmoil of the late '60s. Here was Stafford with his first-person, largely autobiographical poems, violating what I'd just learned all week. He responded generously and without the least sign of annoyance: "Well, it seems to work for me— what do you think?" He was a man modestly confident in his own work (he'd won the National Book Award for Poetry in 1963 for *Traveling Through the Dark*), and so he had no need to puff himself up and rightly reveal what an idiot I was. He did not for a second assume a superior posture and point out that I must not be reading much recent poetry. He knew what a poem was, had just proven the fact for fifty minutes, and was happy to have my own perceptions decide things for me—a mark of a true teacher, as I'd later learn. His example said a poem sang and was human, accessible and resonant, independent of theories, academic or private. It sure worked for me. I was nineteen. Stafford's poem brought back a clear, true moment for me—the blood circling my heart like a July 4th sparkler whipped around in tight circles against the dark, every nerve revving up as I twisted back the throttle on a bike and heard the whine and combustion blast away. This was a sensation I recognized from first riding a motorcycle; this was the sensation I knew I wanted in poems. It would take years to put his gift to use, to take the first step into my own imaginative and real life, hold onto it the way I gripped the han-dle bars heading into a 90-degree turn. But he'd given me a place to start that day, had let me know that my own life could be the stuff of poems. He'd left it idling there in the tall grass for me to pick up when I was ready and, for better or worse, run to the end of my own road.

A long time later, a few years out of graduate school and teaching part time several places, I took my poetry workshop students from

Laguna Beach to Claremont, an hour and a half away, to hear Stafford read. They found his work as clear and thoughtful, even transcendent in its connections, as I always had. I spoke to him afterwards, told part of the story—how he was the first poet I had ever heard and how much it had meant. He seemed to remember visiting St. Mary's College nine or ten years previously, was grateful for my comment, then turned the subject away from himself to a magazine we'd both recently published in. Almost fifteen years later, I'd write to him for poems for a journal I was guest editing, having heard how generously he responded to such requests, and he did.

And a couple years after that I had a gracious short note from him when I asked for one of his much later poems for an *ars poetica* anthology I was putting together. "The Old Writers' Welcome to the New" had appeared in a small literary magazine, the *Cream City Review*, and I thought it one of the best of his many best poems. We weren't paying anything; I had come begging. He responded, saying sure, and also sending others to consider that fit the theme. But I wanted that one and said so, and he gave it to me.

> Glad for this field, welcoming new light,
> we embrace the loss and regret we must pay
> all through our years, that Now may arrive,
> that our story come true and be what it is,
> again and again.
>
> But oh our loves, happy goodbyes.

I think all of Stafford's poems are generous, generous to the earth, to the rest of us, and humble—the poet never more important than the poem, and those are two lessons I keep trying to learn. He taught mainly by example, the good example of his own modest but magical poems. He'd given me the gift I needed—permission to write in my own voice, and he had done it without ever saying so. He gave the bigger gift of the body of his own work, which outshines much, and from which we can still continue to learn.

POLITICS FROM THE '60S

What did I know in 1968? Next to nothing if I'm any judge now. I couldn't have been paying much attention—nineteen years old and attending a small liberal arts college in the woods and hills of Moraga, an environment that was anything but liberal despite being only fifteen minutes from Berkeley. One Saturday in late 1967, some friends and I drove over from St. Mary's College to the UC Berkeley campus to take a test that would tell us whether we would be able to remain in school or would face the draft and the war. The Selective Service System declared that a student needed a score of 70 or above to retain a student deferment. I knew it was an ETS test, the Educational Testing Service who brought us the SAT, the GRE, and a battery of other official exams loaded with math and purposefully oblique questions. They were a business—the more times you had to take their tests to get the required score, the more fees they raked in. Simple. I rode over the hill in silence, in anxiety and anger, feeling that my life had been taken out of my own hands. I came out of the three-hour exam, my head buzzing with timed and meaningless questions about viviparous as opposed to ovoviviparous marine life. But I must have been dealt a test without too much math as I scored a 71. By age eleven I'd abandoned belief in the Catholic Church, but there must have been a guardian angel guiding my guesses that day. That exam, designed to swell the ranks of the conscripted, piqued our political consciousness for a while, yet once it was behind us and we knew we had another two and a half years of college ahead of us, we went back on cruise control.

No doubt we were more concerned about the appalling quality of the food in the refectory or our choice of classes than our elected representatives, the tax dollars draining into Colt Manufacturing, General Dynamics, McDonnell Douglas, DuPont, and all the subsidiaries of the military industrial complex—or those my age dying that day in the jungles of Indochina while we popped open another Burgie draft and chewed the fat, played bridge, or read Aristotle yet again for a philosophy class called "Modern Thought."

Most of us had arrived in college with our parents' ideas and money—there was a connection. In the very early '60s I had spent a year and a half at a private boarding school in Ojai, California—Villanova, a prep school affiliated with the Pennsylvania university of the same name run by Augustinian priests. Though my father was by no means a social climber, the idea of Villanova appealed to him on account of its reputation for discipline and its remote location. My father was conservative—far enough to the right that the then-principal of Villanova would take me out of last period study hall and, with a few other chosen students, sit us in a special room where we listened to weekly tapes by someone who introduced himself as "Colonel Tom R. Hutton, u.s. Air Force, retired." Hutton was somewhere to the right of Atilla the Hun, and although, at fourteen, we knew world history fairly well, we were not then sophisticated enough to make the association. Perhaps the YAF—the Young Americans for Freedom—sponsored the tapes, each one of which began with the admonition, "Know your enemy." It turned out that there were loyal and reasonable people who agreed with "our" position, and then there were Communists, or dupes. Each week, it seemed only a matter of days until the fall of Mexico to a Red invasion across the border.

I was taken out of Villanova when my father did not pay the bills, and so I was spared another semester of those tapes' inflated political doomsaying, opening each week with the oh-so-serious first "da, da, da, dummm" of Beethoven's Fifth Symphony. To say we had been proselytized by the conservative right by the time we arrived in college might be an understatement. We'd heard about Vietnam, but we were going to college, not war. We didn't know who exactly was going—bombastic talk-show hosts on TV kept insisting that they should round up all the hippies and send them. Well, that wasn't us.

But I didn't have both eyes shut. I was vaguely aware the world was undergoing some change when I arrived in Moraga in 1965. The weekend before there had been a big dance or concert—I saw the banners for the Quicksilver Messenger Service and Big Brother and the Holding Company still hanging up over a parking lot on campus. During that first year, we often went over to San Francisco to visit friends from Santa Barbara who were attending the University of San Francisco. We'd walk or hitch a ride to Haight-Ashbury, look at the hippies like the tourists we were, and stumble onto a concert in Golden Gate Park. One time, a side street by the park was blocked off with flatbed trucks—at one end the Jefferson Airplane and at the other Moby Grape. All the same, even there the hippies were a minority in the crowd. Four out of six of us had regular haircuts and wore button-down collars and chinos, although this would soon change. But in those days most of us didn't know Chu Lai from chop suey. We were just tuning into things being very "groovy," happy to be part of a new and developing scene with its kinetic energy and electric music cranking out of the windows instead of soft Beatles' love lyrics. There was an imagery that appealed to our brains, which were just then starting to creak open in the direction of the sky, and perhaps even our fellow members of the human race.

The old order was starting to wobble slightly; even the Beatles would soon shift gears with *Sgt. Pepper's*. We had to take a theology class each semester, and there was a new priest who focused on social consciousness, Father Peter Riga. Given our conservative small college, it was not much of a surprise to hear students call him "Red Riga," but he had some people questioning the status quo for a change. By the start of my junior year, my father had again not paid the tuition and had moved to Arizona. This was actually lucky for me, as my stepfather, Frank Armstrong, was a lawyer who greatly believed in education and the liberal arts, and he immediately picked up the tab. Moreover, I wouldn't have to listen to my father's Neanderthal political perspective on a regular basis. Even with this change I still had quotes from the Stone Age conservative, Dan Smoot, rolling around in my consciousness courtesy of my father. I still wasn't getting things very clear about the war, LBJ, the fact that there were Marine, Navy, and National Guard recruiters in our classroom halls every week. I do, however, remember thinking it was pretty neat when the air force parked a T-15 jet on campus to announce their recruiting presence, and over the weekend a bunch of seniors dragged it from the circle in front of the dorms off into a canyon and covered it tip to tail in toilet paper. Of course it was a big official deal Monday morning when the plane went missing and some FBI types arrived on campus in their dark suits and sunglasses. Things were starting to get interesting.

A few weeks later, a conservative student group sponsored a "lecture" by a Green Beret. With regard to the war, I still had not thought things through enough to boycott yet another military presence on our campus, and so along with my friends Charlie and John I attended the talk, which was held in the little room next to our small bookstore, a room where poetry readings and lectures were usually, if infrequently, held. There must have been a hundred students there, a capacity crowd. And here was the man as advertised—in fatigues, buzz haircut, and still as gung ho as all get-out despite the fact that he was now finished with combat. To us, he was an older man, probably thirty. He had killed plenty of people in Vietnam and was proud of it. And when one student was brave enough to stand up and question the morality of the war—clearly against the political current of the crowd—this guy was ready. He began to talk about how he'd seen his buddies blown up into stew meat, how he'd given talks before where three "subversives" stationed themselves at different corners of the room to make it appear as if dissension was rising from the whole crowd. Then, without missing a beat, he demonstrated how you could roll up a magazine into a tight tube and, with proper placement and thrust, kill attackers in an unarmed situation. I was stunned—what in the world was this madman doing on a Catholic liberal arts campus? It didn't make sense, but some things began to add up for me, and while I did not come out openly against the war—as only a few stalwart souls on our campus would—I could see clearly that there were serious cracks in the official government facade. The Marine recruitment officers in our classroom halls became more aggressive each week, taunting us as we walked by; the body count rose on the nightly news; the whole atmosphere of government coercion loomed more ominously as we approached our senior year.

Late 1967 and early 1968 saw student and citizen protests, marches with a "Dump LBJ" theme. One afternoon, one of my roommates, Pete Cooney, decided to drive over to Berkeley where there was going to be a large student demonstration against the war. Pete was not necessarily opposed to the war and, like most of us then, was still swept along in the national mood, which seemed to support our continued presence in Vietnam. But he was thinking about the situation and, as an amateur photographer, wanted to see some of the action of the times. Pete and a couple of other friends parked their car a few blocks away from the main gate on the Berkeley campus, and as Pete was getting out of the car with his Rolleiflex on a strap around his neck, a big cop was right on top of him pushing his billy club into the lens, backing Pete up against the car, "Boy, if you want to keep that camera, you'd better leave it in the car." Pete, as the cliché has it, weighed 125 pounds soaking wet; he always had a haircut and did not remotely look like a troublemaker. But obviously the police were covering all contingencies; they wanted no documentation. There was the usual crowd control, with tear gas, some of the canisters dropped from helicopters, a few "hippies and left-wing agitators" beaten back with clubs, but nothing was as serious as Kent State would later be or the soon-to-be-infamous Democratic National Convention.

The atmosphere on campus continued to heat up. A group of about fourteen students formed a club they called the November 11th Committee, and by listing themselves as an on-campus club they had the right to have their meetings announced in the refectory along with the other noon announcements. Their purpose was to oppose the war, and just mentioning their presence or the fact of a meeting was regarded as an act of protest against the war. Each time their meeting was announced, even as late as 1969, there was a loud booing from the whole hall. I remember one member of that group, a thoughtful and quiet student named Paul Johnson; we were both English majors. He wore a pair of wire-rimmed glasses, John Lennon–style. That alone was enough in those days to brand him as a radical. He had short hair and spoke clearly and reasonably about morality and about politics, both of which were failing us at the time. Because of his convictions, he was not a popular student in our dorm, and though I'd see him in class, I saw little of him in the evenings. I think often he was acting on his convictions, going over to Berkeley for meetings and marches against the war.

My friends and I were sitting on the fence, amid a campus of comfortable Republicans—after all, we weren't the ones going to go over there and die for what would later be exposed as Westmoreland's lies. But the summer before, my two best friends from home, Steve Schiefen and Francis Orsua, had been sucked into the service, and I'd gone to see them "graduate" from boot camp into Indochina. I had then a double dose of the mentality of the military, and it scared me. I watched guys who had been drafted beating the hell out of each other with pugil sticks to get in shape for war; I listened to the idiocy of the drill sergeants. Then the letters from Vietnam arrived—Steve taking sniper fire while driving convoy near Long Binh, Orsua diving headfirst into bunkers to avoid incoming missiles in Chu Lai. Within inches of their lives. For what? I began to ask myself.

LBJ could feel the country changing—enough so that he refused to run again. He took his record on the war, which he did not want examined in a national debate, his secrets, his bones in the closet, his money, and, as Robert Bly has it, the great "shovel" of his face, and retired to Texas, where he could pull the ears of his hound dogs in peace. I don't think for a minute he felt any real remorse about the thousands of American lives he was responsible for losing, let alone those of a people halfway around the world whose deaths he was responsible for as well. He just made a political decision. As always.

At that time, however, our political consciousness and collective conscience still needed more of a catalyst. How could I have missed the message of the 1968 Democratic National Convention in Chicago? I watched news coverage that had been carefully contrived and was far from comprehensive. How was the average citizen ever to "get it" from just ninety-second sound bites? We relied on David Brinkley and John Chancellor, and the pictures didn't look too bad. Sure there was some disruption, and we were shown some hippies running from the police a couple of times. Subversives, a communist element agitating, Chicago officials were saying. My hair was still short—in retrospect, a political statement, I suppose?

In 1971 I saw *Medium Cool*, a semidocumentary movie about the 1968 Democratic National Convention, in which characters working for a local TV news program were spliced in with actual footage. You saw the training of Mayor Richard Daley's police units, saw them preparing to beat up demonstrators and overrun crowds. The phalanxes of police went through their moves with shields and clubs, the jeeps—barbed wire stretched across wooden pallets affixed to their front bumpers—executed their maneuvers. The documentary footage showed the jeeps driving into crowds of hippies, showed the cops in their light blue helmets chasing down young women and beating them with their clubs, even after they had been driven to the ground. This fascistic display of force was orchestrated by Mayor Daley to deliver the convention to Humphrey. The police and other law enforcement troops were out to safeguard a "closed" convention, to wrap it up for Humphrey on the first ballot, and especially to keep Julian Bond and a delegation of black representatives from Georgia from being recognized and seated. The Democratic National Convention was just a bunch of thugs running roughshod over the democratic process. Some wore suits and gave speeches, and some did the dirtier work behind the scenes and in the streets.

By then I had opposed LBJ and the war, I had supported Robert Kennedy, I was opposing Humphrey and Nixon—what was left to do? Little. As we all know, it was politics as usual, and Nixon won and took years to quit the war. But back to 1968—if the evening news could be manipulated, then how do I know of any thuggery beyond the evidence in the film *Medium Cool*? And of course those pinko-hippie-communist-dupes could have doctored their movie. The answer? My mother's husband, now retired from NBC news and sports, was there.

Scott was working with the Huntley-Brinkley news crew, and they drove their big news trucks into town along a route prescribed by Mayor Daley. As if to presage what was to come, the sides of the streets along the route had been covered up with 4-by-8-foot panels of Sheetrock, some painted and some not, so that no one could see—or point a camera at—the slums along the way. TV crews and delegates were taken on no tours of the city. Once they arrived at the convention center, the crews set about the first order of business, which was power—hooking up the broadcasting trucks to sources of electricity. Although the power boxes had been paid for by NBC, they had been set up by Daley's city crews. When Scott and a couple of other NBC guys went to do the hookup, they were confronted by goon squads, beefy taciturn types dragging lengths of chain on the floor behind them so you could hear it. Ten goons, four or five NBC guys. What are you going to do? They were told that no one was hooking up the power except union members. Powering up is not as simple as plugging in a cord. The trucks had a three-phase power system, and you had to know how to operate it properly or you would burn up vehicles worth about $300,000 each. Scott's crew said they would do the hookup. The goons just stood there, flexed a few muscles, and said "Go ahead," rattling their chains against the floor.

One of the NBC crew members called their boss, Charlie, who said, "Don't do anything"—he must have had some previous experience with Chicago. He arrived on the scene promptly and told the crew just to walk out quietly, saying nothing. They passed through the gauntlet of goons and went back to the hotel, where they killed some time playing cards. The next day a compromise had been arranged—two of Daley's men hooked up the power with the help of an NBC crew member. It was more or less the same deal with camera cables and camera sites; there had to be one of the Chicago guys standing with every NBC crew, at every camera location. Granted, this could have been construed as a union matter. But it turned out that only Daley's men controlled the flow of power to the TV trucks: they were told when and where to hook up and when to cut the electricity off.

As if to underscore the point, the next day, when Scott was in the main studio, the remote unit—a van that drove around the convention site—called in to say that they were having to shut down. Someone had thrown a Molotov cocktail under the van; there was fire, and they had to get out. The driver of the van didn't know who threw the bomb, and, strangely, there were no cops in the area. When the driver finally found an officer, he was told that the police had received a call, and all the available cops had been moved to another location to help control a demonstration. As best they could tell, however, there was in fact no other disturbance to which the cops had been summoned. Basically, there was no security for NBC trucks, although this was not something they could prove. In that situation, though, it sure looked like a message was being delivered. Daley was in control not only of the convention but of how America would see it. That there was independent camera footage being shot, that the networks eventually picked up and broadcast some of the organized abuse by the police—that, as the demonstrators chanted in the streets, "The whole world is watching"—finally didn't faze Daley.

That year, 1968, was the start. The '70s were coming up fast, and by then I would have caught on. Hair length would eventually become a fashion statement as opposed to a political statement, and we would leave Saigon in the autumn of 1974. But the years in between still comprised a good deal of struggle and trials large and petty. Protesting would become a common enough event that it was not always met with violence. My first year out of college I was teaching seventh- and eighth-grade humanities at a Catholic school in Torrance, California—a hotbed of conservatism, as I was to find out. The other teacher hired that year for those grades was Doug Salem, a brilliant man, with genuine social and moral conscience, who would eventually become a dean of a law school at age thirty-one. It was Doug who discovered that Torrance held the largest Armed Forces Day parade of any city in the country, and he was out there on the main street with a poster in each hand, protesting the presence of the army and the assorted tanks and missiles parading through the streets.

I was not brave enough to go out and oppose the masses of the middle class gathered to cheer the defense industry and the pure products of America, although by then I agreed completely with Doug's position. We worked at a Catholic school, and, as I held a minor in theology, I taught a seventh-grade religion class. We listened to some of Bob Dylan's early songs and talked about racism, which was only too evident in Torrance, as the unwritten but thoroughly well-enforced real estate code prohibited houses even being shown to blacks or Hispanics, to say nothing of being sold. To try to engage the teenagers, to give them something they could relate to in a spiritual vein, the songs we sang at mass were contemporary ones—"Get Together," by the Youngbloods, was one they especially liked; it was a hit on the radio then and yet the lyrics were religious and communal. For all of this, as well as for the increasing length of our hair, Doug and I were branded communists by the good parents of the Nativity Catholic School. They held late-night meetings, which they forced the principal and vice principal to attend to hear their complaints. I got a haircut that spring and things seemed to calm down a bit, but my opposition to the war, and to the unfounded and jingoistic justifications proffered by that segment of society, increased.

But it was hopeless to explain all this to my father. In the summer of 1970, I was living in Isla Vista, the student community next to the University of California's Santa Barbara campus. There was a Bank of America in the center of the town, and some radicals threw Molotov cocktails through the windows and burnt the bank down. Bank of America was one of the main financiers of the war in Vietnam, but at that time it was the second largest bank in the country and thus one of the main financiers of anything, good or bad. But it certainly represented "the establishment" and was therefore a target. One reason that all but one of the nine people accused in the attack on the bank were acquitted had to do with an Officer Honey. He was in charge of the police who combed the streets and entered people's apartments without warrants during the three nights of curfew that ensued. Witnesses testified that he told the officers under his command to carry an extra revolver and to throw any gun they used into a fire. There was also testimony that Honey had been overheard saying he was out to get the students and hippies. He carried a medieval mace. His accusations against the defendants did not hold up in court. Of course, a more compelling reason for the acquittals was probably that the police had simply arrested people who were standing around at the time, without any real evidence of their involvement. My friend from both grade school and college, Pete Cooney, was working with lawyers for the defense during the long trial. And my father? He was telling my stepbrothers and sister not to go near Isla Vista, not to visit me—I was crazy. He based this diagnosis largely on the length of my hair and the embroidered ribbon around the hem of my bell-bottom jeans.

What became of those who took the high moral ground in the '60s, who held love-ins and wore flowers in their hair? In the early '70s we managed to elect a few politicians who had a social conscience. In California, we had Jerry Brown as governor for a while, still to my mind the most honest, moral, sensible, and forthright politician to emerge on the American scene. But then Reagan got elected, and Senator Sam Hayakawa, who was as far to the right as Reagan, at least when he was awake for the vote. When gasoline rationing was proposed, Hayakawa suggested that those on welfare—that is, poor people—should not be given a gas allowance as they usually didn't even have cars nor did they have as important places to go as the rest of society. California was turning out politicians in the Darth Vader mode. It seems cynical to say that the baby boomers just became older and had to make mortgage payments, that they had children and bills. I'd like to think that those who became politically aware, who struggled for a more just society, those who saw the necessity of relating reasonably to others in the world and who wanted to preserve the health of the planet, went on to teach, to work in environmental science and research, or to continue to be active politically—that they did not have their ideals undermined by things as obvious as age and economics. But it's hard to find very many examples today. So where did we go? Maybe we were simply supplanted by generation X, by the ethic of conspicuous consumption and $125 brand-name sneakers—the escalation of consumer politics?

Late in the summer of 1996, prior to another Democratic National Convention in Chicago, the CBS evening news ran a special segment about the 1968 convention. They reported that, according to polls taken at the time of that convention, the majority of the public decried the violence and abuse that Daley's storm troopers heaped on those who dared to protest the railroading of the democratic process. Just weeks after the 1996 convention ended, however, the majority of people polled said they approved of the way police had treated the demonstrators. Go figure. As part of the program, CBS also interviewed a professional photographer who had been arrested and roughed up for taking pictures at the 1968 convention, despite the fact that he had all the necessary credentials. He got away with one famous shot, which shows a group of Chicago police officers ready to hit the streets, all of whom have removed their badges and identity tags. There's obviously only one reason you wouldn't have wanted your badge number and ID on you when you waded into the crowds: you didn't want to be identified by your victims. In addition, CBS interviewed a few of the now-retired policemen who worked during the 1968 convention. They said things like, "There was a little bending of the rules," "Those mobs would have ruined the world," "I'd do the same today."

Thirty years later and we still have racism, lack of affordable health care, failing infrastructure in our cities, global warming, contamination of the seas, government by and for corporate America. And yet the essential political struggles of the '60s and '70s, the ideals of truly representative government and personal freedom, barely rate as nostalgia. Given the current political climate in the country, the events and outcomes at home and abroad, anyone who values the struggle for a more peaceful and compassionate world, the genuine idealism that was the heart of the '60s, must be profoundly disappointed—must wonder how, in terms of the development of a humane consciousness, the past forty years can have come to so little.

FLIGHT

I'm walking the cliff over Butterfly Beach where the cypresses lean seaward, or walking the path along East Valley Road from Mt. Carmel Church to Montecito Village, or along the wide sidewalks of Cabrillo Boulevard. I'm younger. Not a kid, but easily younger than now. With three or four friends, I'm just sauntering along, all of us enjoying the autumn light. Then it hits me, mid conversation—I know how to fly!

It's something I'd always known, something I'd simply forgotten until that moment—a little mystical amnesia, a bit of transcendental muscle gone soft that's just come back—and I simply take off into the air, right from the pavement or path. I don't do a Superman or jet-pack kind of fiery streak into the sky. I am not a rocket man; I don't head for the stratosphere. That's not the point. The point seems to be just lifting mildly in my body above the street. I rise a little higher than the level of the palms; I make a loop, some slow turns over a red-tiled rooftop or two.

Coming down—the whole flight is maybe twenty seconds—I'm using my hands to ply the air, a little like dog-paddling in the Pacific, and I set down gently, my arms making a last slow wing-beat to my side. Sometimes, it's a little more frantic and I have to work harder to stay up, cannot rise quite as high. But I nevertheless come close to the light, savor the view, the cloud-spun fabric of the sky. I've shown off a bit to my friends, yet this is something they too know how to do. I was just reminding them. We all walk on together; nothing out of the ordinary has happened.

I had turned forty and was finishing up a new book. One of the only positive things about being exiled to the east with my job was that it helped me find my real subject—my home, my spiritual life anchored in the earth, in Santa Barbara. I had a long poem that combined these flying dreams, homesickness, surfing, aging, and so on, and for a while I felt quite original. Some time later, however, I was reading Dylan Thomas's *Quite Early One Morning*—a remarkable collection of stories, essays, poetry, and prose on poetry—and, about midway through the book, Thomas described the same flying dream. I was not so inventive after all, though I was in good company. I could only hope people did not think I had appropriated Thomas's flight plan.

Not long after, as I was preparing for a reading, I began to realize that not only was I not original with this poem but that my core metaphysical sense, my continuing and unconscious desire for such transcendence, was rooted in *Peter Pan*! Spielberg's *Hook* had just been released, and walking out of the theater, I flashed back to the Golden Book I read and reread as a child, the Disney movie I'd seen umpteen times. Yes, of course, the kid with the nifty hat and feather who had lost his shadow, who could fly—it all came back to me. *Second star to the right and straight on till morning.*

And whom did he hang out with? The Lost Boys—whose anthem was, "I won't grow up!" I was seven or eight, living in the woods of Montecito, and a day, especially in summer or during vacations, was a long, free, and marvelous thing. I was let out on the light's long string and only had to be in for lunch and before the first evening star appeared in the sky. I loved my life—why change? I recalled clearly telling my parents that I did not want to grow up. As far as I could then tell, when kids graduated from eighth grade and headed for high school, they just disappeared from the world—our truly limited, parochial world; we rarely saw them again. I wanted to hold onto my life, and, subliminally at least, I knew growing old was trouble. I climbed up the acacia trees to the sun and felt something in me daily translated into light.

Enter the Catholic Church and Death. We were herded into church almost every other week to sit in the back and pray and stand and kneel for funerals, for people we never knew. Each week, from second grade onward it seemed, another anonymous casket was

rolled down the aisle. The nuns figured that they were banking sanc-
tifying grace at our expense, I guess. We were beaten down with sin
and the hot rocks of hell—death always at the back door. But, outside
of the classroom, I was happy with things as they were. The tide pools
and surf, the loquat with its sun-colored fruit, the nasturtiums nipped
for their nectar; this was as far as I was inclined to carry transcendence. Climbing the oaks and avocados seemed to me what time was
made for, and stopping time seemed like a good idea to the kid I was.

But soon I graduated from Bishop Garcia Diego High School,
and the years shot by like a bottle-rocket sparking against the blue and
seamless reaches of noon. The next thing I knew, the next long slow
breath I took, was to counter academic stress—stress that had my
heart's rhythm lugging in as strained a cadence as a tricked-out cam
in a late-'50s Chevy cruising the four lanes of State Street. I was living
in the east, having dreams of floating around the treetops of the past.

What could I do? How would I hold on? I would write about
growing up and see whether others remembered it the same way. I
did. Some did. My book of nonfiction came out from a university
press back west. It was Christmas, and where was I headed? Home, of
course, to read at bookstores and do a radio interview to promote the
book. Time was short, and I had to fly.

The truth is, I hate flying—much higher than the trees, and you
must give up complete control of your life to save time. But there was
no other way, so I swallowed the Ativan with a vodka tonic and I was
flying. As a boy I was so enraptured with the sun filtering through the
leaves, so content running before the surf, that it was only some vague
specter of death that frightened me, though that of course was never
then clear. For me, airplanes always make it clear.

Going west, we had a bad engine, late takeoffs, and almost missed
our connection—the usual. Southern California had not seen rain for
nine months, but as we lifted off from Denver headed for Palm
Springs we were told to expect turbulence. Clear skies, but a system
was moving in—hundred mile an hour winds in Washington and as
far down as San Francisco—and we were skipping along on its leading edge, bumping all the way.

With the flight delays, I barely had time to visit my mother, borrow her old Mazda, and drive up to Santa Barbara in time for the reading. It was bright and warm until I reached Ventura, then it started to come down steadily. I wondered who would come out in a driving rain just to have a book signed or hear a short piece in which I'm running around in my young life praising the beatific trees. This was the most modest of moments in the local spotlight, and at best I'd hoped to sell ten books, in good weather. This was not about money; there wasn't any. I just hoped not to embarrass myself and the good folks at the bookstore who had gone to the trouble of organizing the evening. But people showed up; some people I had not seen since eighth grade at Our Lady of Mt. Carmel school dropped by and were gracious, chatty, fun. They liked the book—many were mentioned in its pages—and they were eager to elaborate and recall events. There were even some people I did not know who bought the book and liked it for its local knowledge and appreciation of that lost life; this was gratifying and buoyed my spirits a bit despite the weather.

But the best part was seeing my old schoolmates. Yvonne Thornburgh looked very much the same as she did in eighth grade. She had become quite knowledgeable about growing local plants, had been writing and living outside in the sun and air in Summerland, just south of town. But the majority of us looked like our predictably older selves— no Peter Pan luck for us. Terry Mills, whom I had not seen since 1961, told me I had the color of her eyes wrong and talked as if no time had passed; she was relaxed and friendly, gave me a hug, picked up her copy of my book and was gone. As it turned out, I was there for two hours instead of forty-five minutes and never read a word—just signed books and talked with friends who came in. I had no complaints.

Toward the end, high school friends stopped by. We had attended a small school, and members of our class still stay in touch. And although you're not close with everyone, you have your youth in common, a bond of place and time, and, to paraphrase a bumper sticker, you survived Catholic school together. I was almost done signing books and talking with everyone when Pat Tagney and one or two others asked me if I was going to the funeral tomorrow.

There it was again, everything I didn't want. Death, age, loss, rain, the Church, life, afterlife—all the usual suspects called down from the dark skies. I had a radio interview at 8:00 A.M. that next morning. I hadn't been in a church—by design—in years. But Jimmy Hoag had lost his fight of over ten years with MS. I belonged to this group, to this community of which Jimmy was a part. I would be at the funeral.

Jimmy was not my closest friend. Yet in the early '60s, at a small school, you knew everyone, and Jimmy, I remembered, was one of the first people I knew at Bishop. After my father stopped paying the bills at the prep school, Villanova, in the middle of my sophomore year I transferred to Bishop, where many friends from my grammar school had gone and where the tuition was much lower. My friend since third grade, Cameron Carlson, had an old red Studebaker truck, and he took me along to games or dances at the school when I was home, but he would meet up with one of his girlfriends as soon as we were in the doors. I'd met a few kids at the school, and the most friendly and out-going of them all was Jimmy. He always had a new line, gave you a good-natured bad time. He had a huge smile, and lots of high energy, and even though I was an outsider, he came over and talked to me. Yes, of course, an easy enough thing to do, in theory, but we were fourteen and fifteen, and there were the usual cliques, to say nothing of the problem of being a kid from another school. What I will always remember Jimmy for is making me feel included.

Jimmy and I ended up in many of the same classes, and there was a running gag during religion class. We had a rather out-to-lunch teacher, Father Geary, a Jesuit brought in to teach the boys (our school was divided, girls in one half, boys in the other) and who could not manage much else. Today, we'd recognize that he had had a nervous breakdown, but then all we knew was that he kept buying the "confessions" routine. We had at one time been regularly marched out of religion class to the chapel for confessions, a row at a time, once a month. But when that practice stopped, Jimmy and Larry Carol, who always sat by the door and closed it when the bell rang, worked out a scheme to get us out of class. The bell would ring, and Jimmy or Larry would wait a minute until the priest began telling us about the saint of the day and then come in and announce, "Confessions, Father." Father Geary would allow a row out every few minutes, with Jimmy and others of us attaching ourselves from the back and leaving also. After about twenty minutes there would only be eight of the more honest and/or unimaginative students sitting in the front desks, listening to ramblings about the life of Saint Eubaldus—for by that time everyone else knew what was going on, especially when we were going to confession every week, and sometimes twice. Jimmy would pull a ball out of his locker and we'd silently hit the court, the only sounds the bouncing ping of the Voigt and the tinkling of chain nets as the ball swished through.

Jimmy was a bit of a goof-off, a wise guy, but good natured, bright, and you had to admire a kid who could get away with things in a Catholic school classroom and escape the "swats" from Father Salvador and his paddle that those of us not quite as clever received. He became a pharmacist, and would help out charities and the needy, buying medicines at his cost and handing them off to one deserving service or another. He had a terrific sense of irony too, part of his sense of humor, as his older (by less than a year) brother Richie pointed out in his eulogy. Jimmy's favorite phrase was, "This is your lucky day," which, as Richie recalled, was usually delivered at times that would infuriate him—when he'd just gotten a traffic ticket, say, or the day the draft notice appeared in their mailbox. Irony. Jimmy had not had a lucky day in the past ten years. He and I and Sozzi, Schiefen, and Larry Carol were a small group of the youngest boys in our class—somehow those things always surfaced when lining up for a hearing test or health screening. We were the last to have our driver licenses. We were the youngest, had half a year or more on those who were being called up for Vietnam—felt we might have a little longer to face up to things and figure them out.

Jimmy was gone after struggling just to live day to day, strapped in a wheelchair without the use of most of his body. Richie, a veteran of the theater—"In front of God and everyone" as we used to say— tried to explain some of his feelings by retelling the scene from Kazantzakis's *Zorba the Greek* in which Zorba questions his new

British boss's lifestyle. Zorba is looking around his boss's small room at all his books and asks what good books are if they don't tell you why people have to suffer and die. His boss responds, "They tell me about the anguish of men like me who cannot answer questions like yours." Richie and the rest of us were all sinking fast, our hands growing heavy with a lack of answers, a weight we couldn't define. I was conscious of drawing my breath. We were in church, trying to hold onto some belief no matter how immediately unlikely it might seem.

Overnight, the storm had hit full force. Early that morning, north of town in Goleta, I was at a heavy-metal rock station, promoting my book about growing up in the area, between news and surf reports from further down the coast where the waves were "closing out" and surfers were being warned to stay out of the water. Some piers in Ventura had suffered damage. There were leaves and palm fronds in the wet streets, and a galvanized sky beneath which I'd driven to Our Lady of Sorrows Church on Anacapa Street for the ten o'clock service that morning.

No one else was there yet, so I walked around the block a few times. Across the street was the park, the first one my mother took me to when I was four years old and where I played in what was then an old bandstand beneath the shade of palms and ornamental fig trees. I walked past the rectory where I attended receptions for my high school and college friends' marriages. I thought of Tom Neff, who had married Chris Espinosa in this church, married young when we were still juniors in college at St. Mary's—thought of Tom, divorced for a number of years, who two years ago, in deep depression, put a shotgun in his mouth and rode the blast out into darkness.

The day was not going well. The radio interview had been fine; the DJ had read the book, asked relevant questions. A younger sister of Linda Underwood, a classmate from eighth grade, called in and asked how she could get her a copy. But all that finally didn't figure in. How can you add these things up—Jimmy struggling, Tom giving up, the rest of us milling around in our sad suits and ties?

I hadn't been in a church in years. I wanted to avoid the manifestations and dark echoes of that psychologically oppressive atmosphere as far as the future went. I walked around the block again, out to State Street, turned the corner, and there was the Welch-Ryce Funeral Home, where three years before I had gone with my stepmother to arrange for my father's cremation. She had no money left and the man in his sharkskin suit looked down on us for opting for the low-end $1,000 job delivered, essentially, in a milk carton, sans the $300 urn. My father, who always had great health, who made no financial plans, who was basically killed by his allergist who couldn't read the X ray showing pneumonia flooding his lungs like these storm clouds all over the coast—my father, who thought he was going to live forever, who may or may not have wanted a funeral mass, the whole sacramental enchilada, who refused to think about it.

There was no getting around it. When I came back down the street, people had gathered in the vestibule, so I went in and began to visit with folks I hadn't seen in a long while. It was hard even looking at the living. Richard Wesley, a well-spoken Brit whom I had known since fourth or fifth grade, I didn't recognize at first. Always a head of wiry hair, he was now bald. John Donovan, however, was the same— trim, still with all his hair, quiet—but just recently retired (already!) from the air force. How good, I said, that word sounded to me— retired, and at home. And Richie. He was surprised to see me, glad I had come, and we managed a minute or two to catch up. He was strong, organizing things, but clearly shaken. We turned and walked in to the predictable organ music—all shaken.

Our small group of classmates took up three rows on the right side. Pat Tagney went up to lead a prayer—Pat, one of the main movers behind reunions, still had great energy and affection for everyone. Then a relative spoke. There were prayers and the patterned responses of the liturgy. Above to my left, the sky had broken up enough to let the pear-colored sun pour through the western windows. Light fell on the center aisle and the front pews; it was heavy on the stuccoed wall and the lilies and the casket, and dust stood suspended in the shafts of light and seemed to struggle up the air. A good man, a boy happy-go-lucky, cheerful, and then ten years ago, just as suddenly as the sun cut off and the windows greyed, MS. He was courageous, we were told, upbeat until his body was completely defeated.

There I was among old friends, everyone getting too close to fifty. They had been going to church all this time, knew the responses for the Mass of the Resurrection, had a faith it seemed I did not. I remembered a bit of a song and sang with them—and regardless of my disaffection for the Church and its ritual, I was not bitter for being there, for death and the church imposing on me during what was supposed to be a comfortable week at home, for calling my life into question again, for calling all our lives already to account.

Sorrow came in on the light mid-service, burnt steadily there like candle flames, and I broke up—just overwhelmed, more so than I could remember for years. Barbara Schiefen passed me a Kleenex, and I tried to get a grip. This was a funeral of a schoolmate, I knew that coming in. But as much as I liked Jimmy, my anguish was not, of course, all for him. Funerals are not really ever for the dead, excepting the formal service that the devout believe confers grace and helps the soul into the afterlife. Funerals are for the grieving, those who remain. We know this. There I was, forty-seven, and grieving, hard truth be told, for myself, for my friends and that portion of our collective life just taken from us, for the simple fact of so much light having poured through us already and so quickly. And, oh yes, the unlikelihood of salvation, that doubt creeping in with the years, riding bareback on my mortal bones.

Richie concluded his brother's eulogy with a tribute to his courage, his humor, and his sense of irony: "Jim," he said, "this must be your lucky day." I had to stare at my hands for a while, count my fingers and wonder about fate and the random numbers coming up. We'd all gone to funerals for members of our class, a long while back when it seemed especially unjust for someone to be taken so young. But we were young, and going to live, for what felt like—in our charged blood and sinew—forever, and we were going to go through whatever moves, rigors, and transitions necessary to get somewhere, to get hold of a life, a career. Well, now we had. Not finished, but surely there, and now we knew we weren't going to live so long, more road behind us than ahead. I felt pretty pitiful—all of us sad for Jimmy's loss, all of us standing there with little, it seemed to me, but the old phrases to offer up, into the air.

I pulled out of it toward the end. Kathy Ryan's parents had come in the side entrance, and it was good to see her folks still around in their seventies, though they did not go through all the kneeling, standing, and sitting procedures. I was next to my old friend Jim Bret, former oil rig worker now a lay minister. And there was Greg Seaver, who flew in from Arizona just for the funeral, and Jimmy's girlfriend from our senior year, Cynthia Hanzick, had come in from Bozeman, Montana. My old friend Maryann Garland was just in front of me, and we all sang something together, and the last of the light withdrew.

How I longed to be home for good, to stand among all my own— friends who do not read my books or care much that I write them—but in my community, standing there cherishing our life and belonging to one place and time, one group, one thing, loose knit as it was. I wanted to be right there, standing with great sorrow, with great and generous affection, all notes of a chord, a song, singing, sweet Jesus, for our lives and a little happiness among the light and trees and streets of home— a light one of us had lost—and so somehow be redeemed on earth.

They wheeled the casket out and people stood around on the sidewalk for a while visiting, and I talked with Richie a minute again before he organized the cars to go to the cemetery and people began to disperse, to go back to work or to the cemetery for the graveside ceremony. I just couldn't take any more liturgy and death that day. I was trying to find someone to go for a drink—quarter after eleven on a weekday, and what did I care? No one was able to go, no luck, no one to bounce all this off of but myself.

I walked up the side of the church along Anacapa Street to my car and found Maryann parked next to me. We visited a minute more; I asked about her children, her mom, who fed me all through my soph-omore and junior years I think. Maryann had children, places to be. I said goodbye, promising to write, and drove down State Street toward the sea, taking the slow tourist route, remembering the wide four lanes of the old street, driving the single lane now with its stoplights every half block, the sidewalks expanded for shopping. But what did I care now how stalled the traffic was? I wanted to see things, soak it up even if it was all grey. Slow was fine with me.

I moved along unhurried as the clouds and took the new under-pass beneath the freeway out onto Stern's Wharf and parked, deciding to go up to the second-story bar high over the restaurant and pier, sit by the scenic glass window while the wind rumbled by, and watch the lines of surf rise and collapse over the breakwater.

Driving out across the perpetually rickety planks, I remembered how as a child of four or five, I was frightened every time my father would drive us out on the wharf and the loose planks would rattle as we passed over them. I watched the waves crashing in on East Beach, huge breakers for a beach that usually had none. I walked up to the empty bar—midweek, not tourist season, bad weather—and ordered a glass of overpriced chardonnay. There were no surfers out at the sandbar; ten-foot waves rose over the rocks, pounding down on the sand and sending foam high, where it disappeared in the low clouds scrolled across the horizon. I ordered a Bloody Mary and returned to my stool by the window where I could follow the swells as they broke and headed for the beach behind me.

Occasionally, a thin spike of light shot through the squalls and hit a spot on the surface out in the channel. The high surf rolled in, push-ing against the pilings, and I could feel each wave scrape the bottoms of the planks, not far beneath my feet. The pelicans and gulls huddled on the roof of the restaurants, no one flying, nothing lifting into that sky.

FAME AND FORTUNE; OR,
I AM NOT CHRISTOPHER BUCKLEY

Down deep, in the darkest part of the heart, no matter how modest we have become or profess to be, wouldn't every writer—woken in the middle of the night for an immediate yes or no—wish for fame? The most selfless, the most resigned to fate, the most given to *ars gratia artis,* would gladly accept some recognition. Or so I believe after more than twenty-five years' labor in the proverbial fields. What happens when the spotlight glances off the lapels of the glamorous and God-blessed, picks us out one time, standing in the back, hoisting our metaphorical spears? Don't we gasp, straighten our ties, check our hair, and let ourselves believe a bit of that stardust might fall on our foreheads, and, against all better judgment and experience, change our lives? Answer the phone one time expectantly, open the letter mentally rolling the bones as if everyone were due a lucky break, and you're done for. It's almost genetic, systemic, buried in the blood, tugging us away from logic, realistic appraisal, and the plain hard facts of the work being its own reward. Fame, a crumb or the whole loaf, is something we desire even when we say we don't, no matter how strongly we suspect it doesn't *really* mean a thing—spiritually, metaphysically, aesthetically. Just once, we'd like to lay our cards down in the light and clear the table. Most poets I know go to the mailbox the way gamblers go to the casino, the way the hopeless or bereft go to church. Even if they say they don't. They do. Why else send it out? Why not put it all in a drawer with your freezer-burned heart, thereby eliminating all prospects the way that Emily Dickinson did? Given one extreme or the other, most would choose Walt Whitman's route—self-publish and proclaim yourself wondrous before the burning and indifferent universe, the irresolute press.

No one likes loser-clubbers, whiners who begrudge the good they're due. We can't all be stars, logic would dictate. Some writers are tiresome, a host are passable, and even sometimes the truly exceptional are rewarded. Yet marketing and celebrity in America account for most everything—in Hollywood, on Wall Street, or on Main Street. We hate to hear it, but who you know and/or do lunch with counts for a good deal. Imagine that. The same goes in politics, selling T-shirts, or auctioning off the national wilderness to selected oil and mining concerns. My favorite line from Louis Malle's marvelous film *Atlantic City* is, "We don't do business with people we don't do business with." Beyond that, there's just no telling why some are tapped on the shoulder by the angel of fame and given the whole glittering nine yards—regardless of the substance of the writing, or the lack thereof—and others are not. As a beginning writer, you're up against it.

Perhaps the best way to get beyond it is to never really go there at all. Write, publish when you can, but be Zen; get on with the work, cut the complaining, and do the little things you can. Still, some bit of confirmation along the way wouldn't hurt—a letter, a review, a small check or invitation. The extraordinary and original poet Larry Levis wrote, "Anything is enough if you know how poor you are." Larry won some prizes and received a couple grants, but he did not network, did not schmooze or flatter—and who, relative to his genius, is more overlooked than Larry? But what Larry said about modesty, about the essential and ultimate poverty of our vocation, obtains, especially in those moments when we are truly realistic and humble, given wholly to the work—in short, so beaten down by circumstance that we become whatever's next to "spiritual."

Yet as a graduate student writing my first poor earnest poems, wearing my dead stepfather's moth-bitten cashmere sport coat to look as bona fide as possible, I wanted to be acknowledged—if only in the small arena of graduate school writers at San Diego State, if only in a small magazine typed on an IBM Selectric late at night in the office of a furniture-rental store where one of our "editorial board" worked. If we Xeroxed and stapled 150 copies and couldn't give them all away, it was nonetheless important to me to place a poem there, to have an official stamp on my work, even on that pitiable scale.

Fame and fortune elude us early on—choosing up for teams on the playground, class elections in grammar school, sports championships, scholarships, and college prizes—all of which we're sure will improve our lives immediately and into the future. Observation tells us that it's all out there to be had for those with maniacal drive and an unflagging sense of self-worth. And the average writer who gets by allowing the work to be the main thing nevertheless yearns for some approval because he or she believes in the hard work done—the kind of peripheral ambition generally kept in check so that we don't sell out. So even a little regard can get into your blood like a drug and have you making endless comparisons with the haves, have-nots, and shouldn't-haves instead of getting a good night's sleep. Doesn't your spirit sink as you go through all those back pages of awards and grants in *Poets & Writers* every other month? At some point you'd think we would learn from insider trading, or from the flip side of the coin, randomness, and the explosion of contests, and just go back to our desks and dig up anything we can learn about our lives. Finishing my first trek through graduate school, an MA in English at San Diego State, I had no idea how many lessons I still had to learn.

I had sent some early poems to a contest I read about on a flyer on the department bulletin board—sponsored by something like the *College Annual of Poetry*—and one was accepted. In a moment of pride, I mentioned this to my teacher, Glover Davis, who was always candid. He picked out one of the metaphors in the short poem and asked, "You really think that's a good image?" and then smiled a bit sadly. That was it. My first five seconds of fame, gone in a flash. Moreover, he advised me that those college anthology things were usually a racket. True enough, shortly after the highly congratulatory acceptance letter came another asking how many copies, leather bound, of the anthology containing my poem I would like to order at $39.95, which was not small change to a graduate student in 1973. Those companies, they took at least one poem from every sad soul who sent in. I never ordered a book, or even saw one, hoping that since I hadn't come through with the cash, they would drop my miserable poem from the book.

So much for early fame, but fortune was fast on its heels. Three or four months before I was set to graduate, Glover stopped me in the halls one day to ask if I had heard from anyone regarding a scholarship. I said no. I was planning on enrolling in an MFA program in poetry after San Diego State and had no money saved, so a scholarship would be a lifesaver. Glover offered no more details, just a hint of a smirk, and a couple of months went by. Then one evening at my stepsister's house—where I babysat her three kids while she went to night school and where I received my share of poetic support via free dinners—the phone rang and it was the president of the Chaparral Poets of the Golden West. I had, she reported, been recommended by Professor Glover Davis to receive their first-ever college scholarship, and would I be able to attend their convention in three weeks' time at a hotel in San Diego? Dollar signs! I couldn't believe it, but I did, and I didn't pay any mind to the oh-so-poetical name of this group. I felt as if I'd just got a hold of that bad cord on the old toaster, and the air around me was humming with *scholarship, scholarship, scholarship!* Man, was I polite, jotting down times and dates and places and names, thanking the president and what must have been the large panel of judges who selected me from among thousands for this prestigious award!

At the time, it didn't even occur to me that I had never sent in a group of poems to this organization. In the weeks to come I became only marginally dubious as she called asking whether I might leave early on the Saturday to pick up several lady members on my way into town, and would I perhaps be able to come down the night before the ceremonies as well and give a workshop for their members, along with a few other requests that I have now forgotten. I made excuses about people visiting from out of town to get me out of the bus service and the workshop. Still, I was thinking *scholarship* all the way— $500, $1,000, maybe even $2,000. After all, the word was *scholarship*, as in supporting someone who's in school, for a year or possibly more.

Scholarship. I would endure the afternoon, and probably there would at least be a free lunch, and maybe I could duck out early if they began with the college part. Wrong. There is no free lunch. You knew that. I knew very little. It *had* to be worthwhile—an organization with members, a hotel convention, *scholarships.*

Alas, as the old poets said, the scales soon fell from my eyes. I put half a tank in the old Chevy my stepsister had given me, the one with the bad cylinder that gobbled oil and gas, and drove a half hour to downtown San Diego, found the hotel and paid five bucks to park. Upstairs, on the mezzanine, the Chaparral Poets of the Golden West were meeting, the signs in the lobby told me, and up I went to my reward. I was met outside the ballroom by the president and several other white-, silver-, and blue-haired ladies, plus one younger gentleman, in his fifties, who proudly informed me that he had attended the Iowa Writers' Workshop, though he had not managed to graduate. Strategically situated outside the doors were card tables upon which the Chaparral Poets were selling their books, all vanity publications as I quickly came to see. I was directed to one table where the most prominent member displayed crisp, blue, hardback copies of her book of poems about John-John, Carolyn, and Jackie Kennedy after the assassination—a subject she had managed to attenuate through to 1973 and her immediate circle of fame. I was polite—Yes, of course, and Thank you, and How very nice. . . . I did so want to get paid.

The room was packed with children from the local area schools, who had all written poems, and their teachers, who had encouraged them to write the poems and who now would see them acknowledged for their poems. There was a large man with a large voice as the MC, someone I vaguely recollected from my youth pitching products in his baggy suit on local TV channels in L.A. Prior to the ceremonies and the envelopes being distributed to the lucky winners, he announced, we would be regaled with a presentation by the junior high modern dance class from La Jolla School. The curtains parted and fifteen young girls in black leotards fitting too tightly, or alternatively too loosely, teetered on one foot waiting for the needle to drop on the Cat Stevens's album and for "On the Road to Find Out" to blare abruptly over the speaker system. The dance ended with the young ladies tee-tering in their same positions until someone lifted the needle, with a pronounced screech, and the curtains closed. This was just a hint of what was coming.

Following great applause, the MC said they would now begin to announce the prizes, and my slip of a hope was that they would start with the college award and work down. But no. They began with fourth grade. They read the names of four runners-up, the titles of their poems, and the names of their respective schools and teachers. Then they read out the same information for the three winners, and those who'd placed third, second, and first read the complete text of their poems. More applause, envelopes handed out, children bowing into the lights, then on through to the eighth grade, and a break before the high school awards. Sitting near the back, I stole a look around; the large doors to the room remained closed. There was no help. I knew no one and there was no one my age there—just the Golden West's Chaparral Poets and the school kids. Well, I thought, that at least meant they were giving only one college-level scholarship, so enduring three hours of bad poetry and dancing might pay off. Out the few high windows there were no clouds, no seagulls—every-thing out there knew to stay away.

The last event was, of course, the first-ever scholarship award at the college level, and I was called up for an envelope presented by the presi-dent. I smiled, mouthed a thank you over substantial applause, and immediately different groups of the Chaparral Poets came up and put their arms around me, posing for snapshots taken by their friends. One group switched off with the next as I tried to peek into the envelope to see how much the check was for. Someone called to the president, and she walked away just long enough for me to fold back the flap and see what I had come to fear and expect: a check for $25.00.

I quickly tucked it back in the pocket of my dead stepfather's sport coat and began walking down the long center aisle, only to be caught up by the president and the fellow who flunked out of Iowa, inviting me to a member's hotel room to read a few poems and com-ment on the poems of those assembled there. No one knew I had

checked the check, that I knew what a fatuous exercise in self-congrat-
ulation this all had been. They felt they hadn't been found out and so
could continue to prevail upon my good nature, sustained by my gratitude and greed. I lied, saying I still had those guests from Seattle
expecting me for dinner (there had been no lunch or food of any kind
offered during the more than three hours of the ceremony) and kept on
walking out the door, waving politely a Thank you, Thank you, and a
Good afternoon, ladies, I didn't mean at all. Five dollars for gas, five dollars for parking, five hours of a Saturday shot to hell, and the check for
$25.00, which, after expenses, came out to $3.00 an hour for my suffering, for my aspiration to fame and fortune, emphasis on fortune. Like
any grad student, I was on a tight budget, but in this case I would have
paid twenty-five bucks to be able to stay home. Driving back, I did not
think about whether I really deserved a scholarship or not, or about
whether I was just expecting to be lucky, to be rewarded for showing up.
I thought about what Glover used to say about bad experiences, like
getting his bell rung during a college football game: "At least I got a
poem out of it." But this was not the stuff of poetry on either end.

The stuff of poetry did, over the years, keep me afloat, and I managed to publish with little magazines and small presses, for which I
was genuinely grateful. Nevertheless, I kept trying the contests; I sent
in the fees, ate hot dogs and drank jug wine. I had a first manuscript
of poetry by the time I finished up an MFA degree in 1976 and sent it
into the Yale contest—one snowflake in a flurry, as I've often said. My
not entirely unrealistic hope was that my manuscript would do well
enough to draw attention, and perhaps Stanley Kunitz would recommend it elsewhere, which is exactly what happened, so help me. Con-
fessionalism was the rage and much of my manuscript was in that
mode. Kunitz wrote me a postcard, which I've kept until this day, saying that even though I didn't win, my manuscript was one of the final
few among over a thousand and that my poems had "strength, struc-
ture, and dignity." Bless him. That one comment, largely undeserved
it now seems, kept my psyche above water for years. He recommended
my manuscript and one other to the University of Texas Press, and
mine lost out by half a vote. Disappointing, of course, but all writers

need good friends who, as my friend Jon Veinberg's aunt always said, "eat marinated meat and tell the truth." Jon soon had me seeing that perhaps I was fortunate my manuscript had *not* been chosen. I tossed out most of it and started again. At the time, though, I never seriously pondered the possible consequences of the "fame" I would have garnered if that early manuscript had in fact been published. I didn't know my luck, such as it was.

With the manuscript of my third book entered in the National Poetry Series I again came close, or so I heard from a well-connected friend. One of the five celebrated poets selecting books that year had narrowed things down, I was told, to my book and one other. The famous poet could not decide between the two and, the story went, finally tossed a coin. My intuition was always that my friend tried to spare my feelings, as the book selected seemed to be more the style of the famous poet. *Ah, but what if the coin had come up in my favor?* was the question I had to keep myself from asking.

We all have our karma. Mine seemed to be running just out of the money. Nevertheless, I was nothing if not tenacious (read "stubborn"). I kept sending poems off to the magazines in which I was most eager to have my work appear and finally placed two poems in POETRY when John Frederick Nims was editing it. It took several tries, but I got in. Following that, he rejected everything, and after about ten more submissions he brought all of his faculties to bear and wrote saying, "Maybe you're just not writing as well as you used to." Knowing I was pretty disheartened by this, my friend Gary Soto one day asked me confidentially if I wanted to know the secret of getting poems taken at POETRY, where he often published. I said sure, for an instant thinking there might be a secret handshake, a password. "Send good poems!" he replied. He was a pal, and we were used to a bit of razzing. All the same, he had a point. Even to only a modest level of fame, I was ready to take a shortcut. But soon Daniel Halpern at *Antaeus* was accepting poems, and I'd never once been to New York or to one of his fabled dinners. He knew me from no one, and yet he took several poems. What more could you ask? And then Howard Moss at the *New Yorker* accepted a poem, bless his soul. I cashed the largest check I had ever received for poetry, $189.00, and I thought finally I was headed somewhere. I wasn't. And that is where fame and fortune really began to rub my face in it.

Soto, who had published several poems in the *New Yorker,* warned me to expect mail—"People see your poem and write you letters; the magazine forwards them to you." He had received a number of responses to each of his poems, something that rarely happened with literary and small magazines. Sure enough, I received two letters, and that seemed about right—my fame, or lack thereof, relative to Soto's. One was from a divinity student at Yale, which I could not make heads or tails of, and the other, from a divorced mother in Detroit, was entirely surreal. It was 1981, I was teaching at the University of California at Santa Barbara, and the letter arrived in my department mailbox. The Program of Intensive English there was devoted to Equal Opportunity Program students, and there were about seven of us working in it, a friendly and tight-knit group. I opened this letter and began reading things that were so full of non sequiturs that they were hilarious, and so I took it into our little office and read it to my friends, which had everyone breaking up. I should have saved that letter, if only because it seemed so unbelievable, but in my early thirties, I wasn't thinking twenty-some years into the future. The writer began with an indifferent reference to the poem and then went into what I'd had to say about relative language values, and how I would be happy to hear that in her job for the phone company she'd just told a rude customer to "fuck off" and felt great about it; moreover, she had used the same effective phrasing in responding to her belligerent teenage daughter, with similar success. She was also glad, she said, that I had had the lizard removed from my hand—a remark that left me even further mystified. She continued her letter with a series of reports not only unconnected to my life, but unconnected to each other, so far as I or any of my colleagues could tell. There was more, but the specifics are gone with the grey cells of my thirties. It was thoroughly bizarre and made for a good laugh, but more than anything it left us puzzled. The letter was addressed to me c/o the *New Yorker,* so it wasn't a mix-up in the mailroom. I was at a loss.

Later that year, a colleague whom I hardly knew greeted me outside the English department office with congratulations on the poem of mine he'd seen in the *San Francisco Review of Books*. I had no poem there and told him so. "Oh good," he replied, "I didn't like it much anyway." The piece, as I came to discover, was a rather flippant lampoon of Ginsberg's "Howl" that targeted yuppies and was entitled "Yowl." It was written by Christopher Buckley and a coauthor. I had no idea who this other Christopher Buckley might be. But oh, the intimidation that travels with even a little fame. The chance that you might be slightly in the spotlight has people praising your work even when they don't really like it, even when it's not your work!

Not long after that encounter, my friend the Fresno poet Ernesto Trejo sent me a clipping from a recent *Esquire* with a photo and article about the marriage of "Christopher Buckley." The reception looked pretty swank, and a lot was made about how Buckley impulsively, and with apparently genuine exuberance, ate the orchid from atop his wedding cake. Not only did the author of the article comment on it, but Christopher Buckley himself was quoted on the subject of his motivations and reactions and his overall state of health subsequent to this amazing feat. This CB was blond, tall, and thin. Gradually, I began to make sense of things. My namesake was also a writer, son of arch conservative William F. Buckley, and he too had gone to Yale. (My father was William H. Buckley; he had once talked with William F. but considered him too middle of the political road, my father being just right of Darth Vader.) Anyway, in a mad moment of youth, it seems, the other CB had had a lizard tattooed on the web of his thumb, but, as he was coming more and more into the public eye, he had decided to have it removed. He had written a nonfiction book about traveling on a tramp steamer and had done some book tours. At one reading, presumably in Detroit, he must have met a divorced woman with whom had a conversation, which she later took up in her letter where it had left off after she mentioned seeing "his" poem in the *New Yorker*. Mystery solved, but further confusion lay ahead.

In the late 1980s I moved to Pennsylvania to take a job at a state college about an hour outside of Philadelphia, and my location in the east seemed to escalate my identity crisis, the shoulder-bumping with fame that leaves you on the side of the road. The double, the doppelgänger, a long-standing theme in literature, the stuff of movies or surrealist or expressionist novels, was going to do nothing for my career. Right off, the librarian at the university, having received the copies of my books that I had sent, told me that they were mixed in with other books, all under the same name. I began receiving calls and letters in my office. The first of them was from an editor at Scribner's who wanted me to write blurb for a book on the underculture of bodybuilding in New York City. I did not pump iron—they wanted the other guy. I did not respond. I received a second letter saying the deadline was coming up soon. Then came a phone call, one that marked the beginning of what would eventually be years of explaining that I was not Christopher Buckley. The Scribner's editor was convinced that I was the CB she wanted and that I was just trying to get out of doing the blurb, her persistence suggesting to me that the prose-writing CB must hold some sway in New York and/or among bodybuilders.

I later attended a writers' conference in Slovenia, where I met the editor of White Pine Press, a small New York operation. It turned out he was publishing a novel, *Limbo*, written by a friend of mine, Dixie Salazar, and he asked me whether I would be willing to write a blurb for the back cover. I said I'd be happy to, as I was familiar with the book, but I also told him that I could give him the names and addresses of a number of other, much more celebrated writers who would be better qualified to recommend the book than I was. He assured me, however, that he really wanted me to do it. He was a hail-fellow-well-met type and so I sent him a blurb. It occurred to me only afterward that on the back of Dixie's book my words of praise would be followed by "Christopher Buckley." A little publishing deception— and, sure enough, sometime later Dixie reported that people had been asking her how in the world she got someone like Christopher Buckley to do a blurb for her first novel. It then fell to her to explain I wasn't who I was, or however she wanted to phrase it.

Not much time went by before I received a call from someone at NYU about an anthology of short stories he was editing. The book would feature Tom Wolfe, Ernest Hemingway, T. Coraghessan Boyle, and other luminaries. Sorry, wrong guy. OK, do I know where he is? No, try *Esquire*, for which he writes occasionally. Then the editor of a small poetry magazine, who had a new job at the Museum of Art in Philadelphia, called to ask me to read at the museum's "First Wednesday" festivities and to help promote his new issue. He knew who I was, and to prove it he offered no payment beyond a free dinner at the museum. That was the best offer I'd had in a while and I took it. Near the entrance a good jazz quartet was playing and tables had been set up for wine and a light supper; a classic art film would be shown at 8:00. Up the steps to the second floor and far to the back in the dark cloisters was the poetry venue. I was asked to do three twenty-minute readings, with twenty minutes between each, to accommodate the crowds drifting in. Eight or nine people poured into each reading, and after the last one a man came up to me holding a magazine. He was pointing to a fellow in a photo and, looking me right in the eye, said, "You're not Christopher Buckley—he comes in for gas to my dock in Connecticut every summer on his yacht." "Oh, so that's what happened to my yacht!" I wish I'd said, but holding up a book with my name on it was my only response.

It went on. A note from Charles Simic—a wonderful poet, born in Belgrade—saluting me on my essay in the *New Yorker*. I'd exchanged a few letters with Simic regarding a visit to Yugoslavia I'd made on a Fulbright fellowship and the poets I'd met there. He was very kind and had sent me a copy of his translation of Aleksandar Ristovic's *Some Other Wine and Light*. It just felt like very bad manners to write him back to correct his mistake—to explain that it was the other CB now writing little essays for the *New Yorker* and *TV Guide*. I'd also been publishing the occasional poem in the *Sewanee Review* and at one point had a phone conversation with the editor, George Core, who announced, without compunction, that he really didn't like the piece I'd written for *Esquire* on Vietnam. That time I was happy to explain I wasn't Christopher Buckley. Not long after that I received a call in my office from an editor at *Esquire*, asking for my address. Once I straightened him out on who I wasn't, I pointed out that since the other CB wrote for them, he should be able to check the files there. My friend and former teacher, Diane Wakoski, suggested I use my middle initial to halt the confusion, but I'd been publishing since 1974 without it and didn't feel I should have to change things now.

The most memorable mix-up, however, occurred a few months before the Clinton-Bush election. The phone rang at home one Friday morning, and it was the woman who coordinated guests for the *Today Show*. Very deferential—Can you talk now? Have I caught you at a bad time? She didn't say exactly why she wanted me on the show, but she was pushing me to commit to an appearance. I explained that I was a poet; she said she knew that and had obtained my home phone number from Vanderbilt University Press, where two of my books had been published. Yes, I replied, those are my books, but you are looking for the other guy. No, she declared emphatically, she wanted me to be on the show next week. By this point, I had already learned that the other CB had been a speechwriter for George Bush, and my politics were 180 degrees different from his. Without too much imagination, I could see that she wanted me/him to offer an insider evaluation of the candidate. She was obviously used to people dodging requests to appear, and so she kept after me until, finally, I offered an evaluation of Bush and the Republicans—something about Irangate, lying, and the selling of America, as opposed to honoring the social contract of government—that finally left no doubt in her mind that she had the wrong man, and she hung up before I finished.

In 1996 I received a very nice invitation to read at the 30th Annual Sophomore Literary Festival at the University of Notre Dame. The letter came to my department office in Pennsylvania; a young woman with the very horse-and-hounds name of Hunter Campaigne was the chair of the event and seemed to know who and where I was. I was asked to give one reading and a workshop, the cost of accommodations would be covered, and "an honorarium is negotiable," the letter said. I figured the cost of a rental car and driving time, as I hate to fly, and wrote back to accept, saying that I would need at least a $500 honorarium. I looked at the list of past participants and could see I would be among the great and the glamorous—Diane Wakoski, Tim

O'Brien, Gwendolyn Brooks, Tobias Wolff, Sharon Olds, Galway Kinnell, Derek Walcott, T. Coraghessan Boyle. But there were also a few folks closer to my level, further down the ladder, and one or two I had never heard of. It was me they wanted, I told myself. If I'd read back further on the list, to the late 1960s, I'd have seen the names William F. Buckley Jr., George Plimpton, and the like, and the buzzer would have gone off in my head. But I didn't, it didn't. Then I had another letter from Hunter Campaigne saying that she would need a CV and a current photo before she could finalize my appearance at the festival. I was currently out of photos but sent the CV, and I never heard from her again. The deal killer, I realized, had been asking for the $500—not too much, but too little. They wanted the author of the light novels *The White House Mess* and *Steaming to Bamboola*. The famous don't show for $500.

In 2001, I received a second National Endowment for the Arts grant in poetry. Speaking with the coordinator after she gave me the good news, I was told who the judges were, and my immediate response was, "Someone made a mistake." I couldn't believe that the poets on that list would choose my work, poetry politics being what they are. But the panel of judges was larger than it had been in the past, and so not every judge read each poet's work. Some angel had guided my manuscript past the hands of those with agendas and into hands of more receptive (or, I like to think, more objective) judges— into the hands of fortune, for a change. The woman at the NEA knew I wasn't the other, better-known CB, and she was kind enough to relate the story of the final meeting, during which the coordinator matches the winning manuscript numbers to their respective authors' names—for the proceedings are truly anonymous these days, with the possible exception of judges who recognize a student's or friend's poems and do not recuse themselves. In any event, when she matched a number to "Christopher Buckley" there was, she said, an audible groan, the NEA judges thinking that they had awarded a poetry grant to the Christopher Buckley of *TV Guide* articles and the novels *Thank You for Smoking* and *Little Green Men*. When she explained that I was not that CB, they breathed a proverbial sigh of relief, she told me. For once, not being Christopher Buckley landed me in fortune's lap.

A year later, and had the NEA changed my life? No. Notoriety turns fortune's wheels and unlocks the coffers, and depending on your income bracket, you will give a quarter to a third of your grant back in taxes. But the money sure keeps you going, is acknowledgment from your peers, and enables you to repair the car and write over the summer without taking on extra work. In short, it enables you to keep on doing what you love. Much gratitude, no complaints. But then came the capper. In December 2001, within the space of a single week I suddenly received a number of emails from friends and letters from relatives congratulating me on finally reaching the ranks of the truly celebrated. "I know the National Book Award would be great," a poet friend wrote, "and a MacArthur even better, but you can't go wrong being part of the final *Jeopardy* answer, as you were the other day." A former student, someone I hadn't heard from in twenty years, also emailed after watching the show. I had not seen it myself, but it turned out that the final answer for the contestants was something like, "Famous American painter about whom Christopher Buckley wrote the book *Blossoms and Bones*." And the question was, "Who is Georgia O'Keeffe?"

I knew that quiz shows sometimes throw in a question about poetry at the high levels to stump contestants—they know that Americans read very little poetry. I remember having dinner at my mother's one evening and watching *Who Wants to Be a Millionaire?* and the question that stopped the contestant at the half-million-dollar mark was, "Who is the current poet laureate of the United States?" As it happens, *Blossoms and Bones* actually is my book, not the other Christopher Buckley's. But the folks who write the questions for *Jeopardy* probably didn't realize that. Moreover, as I was well aware, the other CB had some cache with NBC, *TV Guide*, and a number of glossy magazines, and libraries and Internet sites often jumbled our books together. It was not difficult to figure out that some devious researcher had assumed that the book was by the other Christopher Buckley and that he was famous enough to mention in a quiz-show question. *Sic gloria transit mundi.*

I did find a little satisfaction recently, however, when searching for two of my out-of-print letterpress books at the library, on the

Internet. I gone to ABEbooks.com, a wonderful Web site that lists hundreds of bookstores and booksellers in the U.S. and Canada. This was one of my first times at the site, and instead of typing in a particular title, I just typed in my name, and something like 870 books came up. Major poets such as Philip Levine might have a thousand listings; Tim O'Brien might have twelve hundred. Out of curiosity, I plowed through all 870 and, way back somewhere in the 700s, I found one copy of each book I wanted. Perhaps thirty of the books listed for sale were mine. Twenty or so were by a British Christopher Buckley, who wrote books about World War II military strategy. Roughly eight hundred, then, were copies of books written by the other CB; despite his celebrity, it didn't seem that many people held on to them. I was happy to pay some high prices for my two rare, beautifully printed books, content with my relative fortune and fame, even though I wasn't Christopher Buckley.

POETRY AND POLITICS

In the third edition of his creative writing text, *Three Genres*, Stephen Minot offers good advice to the beginning writer. Essentially, he says that if you visit New Mexico you may have some material for a piece about a tourist in New Mexico, but you should not try to write about the life of a Navaho on the reservation. I, then, can write about my impressions of the former Yugoslavia only as a tourist—a guest of the state, to some extent, and the guest of poets for six weeks during the spring and early summer of 1989. I was awarded a Fulbright grant in creative writing, and my primary function was to exchange views of poetry and writing with writers throughout the country and to attend, as the u.s. representative, the two major writers' conferences, Sarajevo Poetry Days and the PEN conference in Slovenia. I had, only in the few years previous to my trip, become familiar with Yugoslavian poets, but I knew little about the politics of the country at large and the ethnic areas within.

At first, I encountered poetry more than politics, but both were equally on my mind after only a week in the country. In the few months preceding my trip, there had been a number of news reports about "unrest" in Kosovo, the southwest portion of Yugoslavia, which has a high concentration of ethnic Albanians. The national army, under orders from Belgrade, had gone in to put down demonstrations and some Yugoslav Albanians had been shot. Although I occasionally asked openly about the situation in Kosovo, my impressions came mainly from what I overheard in conversations, and also from what many poets and writers simply wanted to avoid discussing. By the time I left from the Split airport in June, I had a sense of the political climate via the Serbian central government in Belgrade, and Serbian aggression during the final months of 1992 and into 1993, and ultimately through 1995, substantiated that impression. I would have preferred my views to have been wrong; I would have preferred to concentrate on poetry.

I had heard wonderful things about the Fulbright program in Yugoslavia as early as 1984 from the poets Diane Wakoski and Susan Ludvigson, who visited that same year. Later, Larry Levis and Philip Dacey, among other well-known writers, went over, and by all accounts it appeared to be an interesting and energetic program. From reading and conversations, I knew of the beauty of the Dalmatian coast and the intriguing Stari Grads, the old towns, of Sarajevo, Dubrovnik, and Zagreb. I was aware of the many fine poets working in Belgrade and Slovenia and had also heard about the warmth and hospitality of the writers' center in each city and the weeklong poetry festivals. Certainly, the climate for poets and for writing generally in Yugoslavia seemed to far surpass anything in this country. I applied to the program twice and was accepted on the second application— largely, I think, through the influence of Richard Jackson.

I had gotten to know Jackson at the Bread Loaf Writers' Conference in 1988, when he and I were paired to respond to a dozen or so manuscripts by contributors. By that point I had read Vasko Popa and Ivan V. Lalic in the Charles Simic translations. A few years earlier, Jackson had been to Yugoslavia on a Fulbright and had gone back since then. As editor of the *Poetry Miscellany*, he had published a special feature on Yugoslavian writers and was passing out copies at the conference. He had also brought along the Ecco Press's *Selected Poems* of Tomaž Šalamun, the great Slovene poet, and over the two weeks showed me many of his poems. I found all the work exciting, especially Šalamun and Lalic, who seemed to me so much more accessible than Popa, the Yugoslavian poet with whom Americans were most likely to be familiar. There was still the characteristic use of myth, along with a little riddling, still the elliptical imagistic sequences, but to my reading the psychological and personal motivations for the imagery seemed clearer and more moving in these poets than in the more medieval strategies of Popa. Also I started to read newer poets such as Boris Novak, Veno Taufer, Aleksandar Petrov, and Mario Suško. Rick had be-come something of a transplanted local hero in Yugoslavia. In addition to the special issue of the *Poetry Miscellany,* he was going to pub-lish several chapbooks of Yugoslav and Slovene poets in translation and was returning there for the third summer in a row, bringing students along with him. He would be presenting demonstration poetry work-shops at the university in Sarajevo and the PEN conference in Slovenia, as well as arranging for Yugoslavian poets to visit the United States. When it came to my second application for the Fulbright, my increased familiar-ity with the poetry and poets of Yugoslavia, coupled with a letter from Jackson, turned the trick, I think.

Jackson was, moreover, instrumental in setting up an itinerary for me during my visit. Despite numerous cables, letters, forms, etc., there seemed to be no actual communication between the Fulbright offices in Washington and in Belgrade. Rick knew the dates of the two big conferences and was in touch with the organizers, and he let them know that I was the poet selected for the Fulbright program and that I would be attending. In between the two major events, I was on my own to arrange transportation around the country, visits with writers, readings, and such. Rick was bringing a group of students and attend-ing the same conferences. I arranged to travel with him and set up my schedule accordingly.

Washington did say that I should be in Belgrade by the end of April—something about formally presenting myself to the Fulbright office there and to the writers who had contributed to my selection. So I arrived, after thirty-seven straight hours of travel, to find no one at the airport to help me find the correct bus into town or the hotel where I had a room reserved for me. I eventually found the Hotel Kasina after a half hour of walking around the downtown area with my bags and was shown to a small, spartan, proletariat-type room. The Kasina was a state-subsidized hotel. You could, of course, stay across the street at the charming Hotel Moscova; you could pay for it yourself. No sleep in a day and a half, about four words of Serbo-

Croatian: I stayed put. I pushed open the French windows the six inches they would move, wedged my shoulders between the window frames as best I could, looked out over the street, and then went down and sat at a table on the sidewalk as the late afternoon light dusted down over Belgrade. I drank slowly a tall local beer, went up to my room, and slept until midnight, when I woke up, read for a while, and went back to sleep until 9:00 the next morning. I had no idea what would come next.

I had arrived with only one day left to contact the Yugoslav Fulbright office—half a day, really, as the director, Bojan Drndić, was leaving early to drive to his house on the coast for the holidays. It was both May Day and Easter weekend, and everything would be closed for days. Jackson would not arrive with his crew for another week. I did finally receive a call from the u.s. assistant cultural affairs officer, who said she would try to put a dinner together so that I could meet some folks. But it was a bad time to arrive in town, she said—this holiday weekend by which the embassy had insisted I arrive. Did these people talk to each other? I wondered. She went on to say that she had worked out a schedule for me, something I had been expecting to receive for months. By this point. I told her, I had of necessity arranged my own schedule, and I would keep to that. I did manage to add on a reading and presentation at the old library in Dubrovnik toward the end of my stay, which was very rewarding, although I was unable to coordinate with some poets in Zagreb who were evidently interested in my work. As for Belgrade, we were in luck in that a number of writers had remained in town. At a very nice dinner at her very nice home, the assistant cultural affairs officer introduced me to Ivan Lalic, Aleksandar (Sasha) Petrov, and a number of other interesting writers and local Belgrade people. Lalic was a modest, somewhat reserved man, wearing a conservative business suit and tie. He was generous about my own poems and relaxed in speaking about his own, although, again, he did so very modestly. I knew his bright, brooding, and gently surreal poems from *Roll Call of Mirrors*, the translation by Charles Simic that Wesleyan University Press had published the previous year. Petrov was very outgoing and personable and had a sheaf of his recent work that he was handing around. He and his wife, Krinka, a prolific translator, invited me out to their home in the suburbs for dinner later that week.

For the next four days, I wandered on my own around Belgrade. It was a cold late April and early May, and I was lucky that at least the bars remained open; most of the other shops, notably all those along the great pedestrian mall in the heart of town, were closed for the holidays. With the locals, I promenaded up and down the mall, hour upon hour, looking more at the people than in the shop windows. I checked to see when museums would be open and visited the painting and archeological exhibits. I walked out of town across the river to the Museum of Modern Art, but it was closed. Mostly, though, I walked back and forth along the mall and out and back to the great public park in the old Roman fort of Kalemegdan, where I watched the grey waters of the Sava and the Danube converge below the equally grey sky. I took a new route through the park each day and also found a small park, a little square really, off the main pedestrian mall, where I would go after an hour or so of walking to escape the coal smoke that oiled the air. Usually, no one was there but the magpies and one very old man who shuffled along the paths among the pale irises, a man who had been there before the communists and seemed determined, in his constant movement, to outlast them.

A portion of the park at Kalemegdan was filled with World War II displays of cannons and tanks, plus one boat with grey paint and wood peeling off. But I began to notice something else—a preponderance of young men in army uniforms. They all had new shoes and the same olive-colored wool coats, which were thick as blankets. They were everywhere, in groups of three to six or seven, young men eighteen or twenty years old. It seemed that they were all on furlough for the long weekend and had ended up in the same place. Each day at 4:00, the time until which I made myself stay outside walking, I headed for a nice bar overlooking the small square at the end of the mall and ordered a lovely great bottle of the local Belgrade beer and a slivovitz. I'd make notes in my small book, sip the slivovitz and half the beer, and then order one more slivovitz. The chill disappeared, the thermodynamic mists of the slivovitz rose inside me like the sun out of the sea, and I did not feel sorry for myself there in a foreign city quite alone, unable to speak with anyone besides hotel clerks, waiters, and workers in the bar. The soldiers crowded the tables and shared drinks, two or three to a beer or Coke, and seemed to be having a fine time. They smoked the government-subsidized cigarettes that cost about thirteen cents a pack—everyone smoked, at all times, in all places—and when they finished drinking, they would go for another stroll up the promenade or stand in line for the one movie theater.

One day I walked in a direction away from the park and into the business district, as a waiter in the hotel had told me that one or two small groceries would open for an hour or two around midday and I needed a bottle of wine to take to Sasha and Krinka's for dinner. Even walking away from the mall, I ran into groups of soldiers on almost every street. I assumed that they were all stationed in Belgrade and were allowed to be out all day for Easter and May Day. I got a bit lost, as the street signs were all in the Cyrillic alphabet, but then I hadn't much else to do, and I did want to find a store that was open. I came across one by chance, a small "mom and pop" type store, and there was a line, which gave me time to practice my three words of Serbo-Croatian, which I hoped would result in a nice bottle of wine. There were only two kinds of wine on the shelf, both with metal caps, the kind you used to find on old bottles of Coke. I pointed to the one with the more interesting label, paid the equivalent of about a dollar, and left to some strange looks from the local neighborhood folks; my dress and speech were clearly out of place.

I had met Lalic, which had been one of my hopes for Belgrade, along with some other very engaging writers. But none of the poets, and certainly not the assistant cultural affairs officer, had mentioned Kosovo. I had the example of the soldiers everywhere around me, and yet no one spoke of politics. On May Day, as I was walking through the hotel section of the city, I heard some booming choral music next to the main Marx-Lenin square. I stood on the edge of the park with a few older people—for all I could tell, the only tourist—and watched what was going on over at the old government building. One camera was set up on a TV truck across the street from the entrance to the building, black cables straddled the street, and the road was blocked off. Banks of speakers were installed on each side of the steps up to the main entrance, out of which what was surely a grand chorus of some sort of "People's Ode to the State" burst forth. After about five minutes the doors opened and groups of teenagers, waving flags and mouthing the words of the song, rushed out beneath the pillars and ran to two flatbed trucks stationed on either side of the entrance. The TV camera held its one unwavering position as the energetic teenagers climbed upon the beds of the trucks and were driven back and forth in front of the camera, waving flags. It was all orchestrated to look as though a large celebration was taking place. The local people there, like me, had perplexed looks on their faces, which soon changed to indifference as they hoisted their shopping bags and headed off through the park or down the sidewalk. This official posturing would of course turn up on the one TV channel that night as news. Across the square, four large flags hung down the face of the modern, high, cement government offices—one with a picture of Marx, one with Lenin, one with Engels, and one with Tito. No one looked up. I walked across the street toward the post office, and in my beard, jeans, old blue jacket, and black shoes I must have looked enough like a local that a woman stopped me to ask directions. I thought it a good bet that someone in from the countryside would not speak English, so I replied in Spanish, a language I command slightly better than Serbo-Croatian, saying I was sorry, I didn't know. I headed through the park wondering about the Yugoslavian Communist Party. Who belonged? No one appeared to really much care. The teenagers had obviously been hired, or otherwise coerced, and the TV crew, their status as instruments of the socialist state notwithstanding, knew how to produce commercial TV that would fill in the wide gap of political apathy.

I acquired a more immediate sense of how the Party could operate, however, through my dealings with Bojan Drndić, the director of the Fulbright office, at which I duly appeared the following Tuesday, when things returned to normal. He was dressed in a stylish suit and had had a wonderful holiday on the coast, at his second home. Drndić was fairly high up in the Party, and his office boasted a computer and copier, secretaries, an accountant behind closed doors, and a nice coffee machine. On the shelves, I saw dozens of copies of poetry books by a number of poets who had visited on the Fulbright program—books obviously never distributed. He had learned his English in Washington, D.C., the son of a diplomat. His idioms were so swift, exact, and up to date, he was so slick, he could have sold a used car to Richard Nixon. He was in charge of the Fulbright program and my visit, but he had done next to nothing about it. I had to talk to him about an itinerary, formal requirements, hotel reservations, my stipend for travel. Nothing had been arranged along these lines, not much information was available, but he assured me that it was all "no problem"—he would take care of all of these reservations, etc. I was in and out of the office in twenty minutes, my official presentation of myself to the Fulbright commission and the Party complete. He did in fact secure two airline tickets for me for upcoming trips at the Yugoslavian rate instead of the tourist rate, which would have been three times the cost, but that was about the end of it. Luckily, the assistant cultural affairs officer at the embassy had made a reservation at the Hotel Europa in Sarajevo for me, as that part of my itinerary and her belated one happened to coincide.

While I was at the Fulbright office, Drndić went into a back room and reappeared with an envelope stuffed with Dinars. It was thick enough to choke the proverbial horse, but it was only about one-fifth of what he was supposed to provide, what would be necessary for expenses. No problem. He would wire the rest to the hotel in Stan, or Dubrovnik, or Sarajevo—it kept changing each time I talked to him from a public telephone office, and the calls were not cheap. The Dinar was suffering weekly inflation relative to the U.S. dollar, and so Drndić would put me off, a week at a time, wiring only a portion of my funds—just enough to get me out of one town and on the road to the next—at the previous week's exchange rate. Presumably he pocketed the difference, either for himself or his office, to say nothing of eating up a good portion of my time in each of the cities I visited as I chased around after his bureaucratic paper trail. Lying—diplomatic speak—was part of daily business routine for him. Time and again I was told that my stipend would be at such-and-such a place and that the full amount would be sent. It never happened. In Ljubljana I went to the American Center for help, and the Slovenian woman who worked in the office called to Belgrade to find out what had happened to my stipend. I was sent to a post office across town for it: no money. I came back the next day, apologized for being a nuisance, and she called again. This time it was a different post office: only a partial amount. I returned, she made a third call, looked at me, and said something in Slovene that translated "Serbian business!" Again, at the hotel in Lake Bled, no stipend had been wired as promised. Three more phone calls, daily checks with the desk clerk—nothing. On the last day, there was a message regarding the remainder of my stipend, without which I would not be able to pay the hotel bill. I had to hire a cab to drive me over to the next town, where I was obliged to go to three separate offices and sit through three sets of interviews before I was finally able to pick up my last bit of money. This cost about $25 and took up most of my last morning at Lake Bled.

Drndić made a good profit off me, and I imagined him chuckling to himself each time I called in. Ah, the prerogatives of power, political privilege. Only about 20 percent of Yugoslavs belonged to the Communist Party, I learned, yet it could provide you with an easy job you could do or not do, two houses, a car, nice suits, and the ability to skim a little off the top. Party officials—a number of whom we met at various state receptions in lavish government buildings situated along Lake Bled—seemed to me like well-to-do members of Congress or prominent Republican Party appointees. But I get ahead of myself.

In Belgrade, I enjoyed a cordial and stimulating evening with writers and poets, but, again, no one mentioned Kosovo. At the home of Aleksandar and Krinka Petrov, I was treated to Sasha's homemade lemon and hot pepper vodka, wonderful Serbian cuisine, and talk of poetry and translation—a wonderful evening with generous and gracious hosts. We talked about Spanish poets—García Lorca, Hernandez, Machado, the Generation of '27. Krinka translated a good deal of poetry to and from Spanish and was off soon again to Spain for another conference on poetry in translation. Still, all the boys in uniform all over town—I wondered. Nor was anyone much concerned with the Albanian question. Perhaps they simply felt there was nothing they need be concerned about—? Or perhaps Kosovo was just small and far away and the army would of course keep things in order. At the same time, no one was eager to embrace the official state position or its outward political trappings: the May Day "celebration" was hardly that. I saw more people attending the rich and sonorous Easter-week ceremonies in the big Russian Orthodox church or sitting outside the city's most famous bar right across the street, where you could still hear the chanting and smell the incense.

Rick Jackson and his crew arrived the next day, and we rented vans and headed for the town of Stan on the coast, not too far from Dubrovnik. Stan was a small village founded to support the frontier wall of the ancient kingdom of Ragusa, which stretched south to Dubrovnik. The wall still worked its broken way over the considerable hills, and some students one night fearlessly walked its vestigial reaches. All of us strolled along the wall surrounding the old city of Dubrovnik. You paid a nominal amount to climb up to the path at the top of the wall, and it was a wide and wondrous view from almost anywhere. The small harbor was tucked away from the sea in back of the wall, and you could easily see how in feudal times the location would have been well protected from invaders by land or by sea. At this point we were really tourists, enjoying the sights and seacoast and the enticing food and wine—the local fish grilled in garlic and oil with a lovely bottle of white Graševina, the roast veal and potatoes accompanied by the spicy Blatina from Mostar or a rich and complex bottle of Posip. One night we attended a superb chamber orchestra concert in the baroque church, featuring Bach, Albinoni, and Mozart. We traveled to Split, where we took in a performance of Mozart's *Requiem*—a full choral group and orchestra, all from Split, and performed in the Split opera house. The tickets cost us about $1.50. Besides Split, we visited Trogir, also on the beautiful Dalmatian coast, and then made the long drive to Mostar to see the old city. We visited the mosque and ate at a wonderful outdoor restaurant, the food somewhere between Greek and Turkish. We also visited the most famous landmark, the high arching stone bridge across the river. Later, at a bar, we met an architectural student from the States who had come to Mostar to study the bridge. He was making a model, and, as it turned out, his parents were from the area. It was not clear to us precisely how old the bridge was, but centuries ago an Ottoman sultan had ordered the bridge built, only to have it collapse. The surviving bridge had been constructed after the sultan told its builder (or so the story runs) that he would live as long as the bridge held. Only a few years later I would turn on the TV news to see the inhabitants of Mostar—Croats and Muslims alike—piling layer upon layer of old tires, held together by ropes, over the side of the bridge in a futile attempt to repel the shells that the Serbs had aimed at the bridge for no reason other than to humiliate the inhabitants by destroying their landmark. The bridge was really only wide enough for carts and people and so was of no significant military importance, and the Serbs destroyed it.

We did not meet any writers until we returned to Sarajevo for the weeklong 27th annual Sarajevo Poetry Days festival. Rick and I each read a poem at the international session, at which many major countries were represented. Poets read in their own language, and then an actor would read the poem in Serbo-Croatian, or Croatian-Serbian as they referred to it. There were late-evening readings by poets from individual countries as well—evenings of Italian poetry, Austrian, German, plus a bilingual reading and discussion of American poetry organized by our host, Mario Suško, in which Jackson and I participated along with Stephen Dobyns, who was on a USIA visit for a week or two. But by far the majority of the poets were Bosnians and Croatians. One night, largely out of respect for our host, Jackson and I sat through an hour and a half of poetry entirely in Bosnian, even though between us we knew only enough words to order beer and ask directions to the hotel. We were, nonetheless, able to tell the formal poets from the free verse.

Mario Suško later escaped Sarajevo and now teaches at a community college on Long Island. I had first met him at an outdoor café in

Sarajevo, where the talk was of translation, poetry, and the relative absence of politics in publishing, at least from his perspective. At age twenty-four he had translated Whitman's "Song of Myself" into Serbo-Croatian, and the only question the editor of the literary magazine that published it had asked him was whether it was good stuff. There were no questions about what dangerous American ideas might lie behind the poem. Nor did any of the Yugoslavian poets at the festival speak of the political unrest. There were no Serbian poets in attendance, and few Slovene—the former absence was the result of poetic jealousy, I now suspect, and the latter probably political tension. Nonetheless, it was truly refreshing to see how much goodwill there could be between so many different poets from different countries. There was a poet from Cypress, and one from Egypt, Poland, Czechoslovakia, Austria, Italy, and more. Not all was perfect, however. The Russian poets were for the most part distant and formal (they read in the old, stentorian mode), and there was an arrogant and egotistical poet from Iraq who put everyone off. There were surprises too. We met the Russian poet Vyacheslav Kuprianov, leader of a new free verse movement there, and the Cuban poet Excilia Saldaña, who had a great lyric and imagistic gift. Still, we did not discover much political discussion. If, as Shelley claimed, we poets were legislators, we were truly unacknowledged.

We did get some discussion going, however, when I worked with Jackson and his students to present an American-style poetry workshop at the university in Sarajevo. The professors were a little skeptical, but interested. In Yugoslavia, as in most of Europe, if you were a writer you just got on with it and wrote. At some point you either made it, or you faded away. As far as I could tell, no one was eager to critique another writer's work. Writers moved in much smaller circles, each city having its own group. While the idea of a "teacher" of writing was essentially a foreign one, it did seem some poets had mentors. As I later came to see, the well-known Slovene poet Tomaž Šalamun championed the younger poet Aleš Debeljak. And one of the things I found most heartening about all the Yugoslavian cities was their writers' union, which gave support to writers at all levels. Each major city had a building dedicated to nothing but the area's writers. There was often a restaurant, as well as a bookshop, a general reading room, and rooms for seminars. Visiting writers were brought there to meet with the director and other writers; you could have a glass of juice or a beer and talk about your work. The writers' union also published books by local writers. It was the most civilized approach to writing, the most systematic support for art, I have ever seen at the state or social level. We could do well to learn from that example.

Once or twice during the Sarajevo festival, aside from all the readings and gatherings, I would asked a writer officially connected with the event and/or the writers' union about the government in Belgrade and the situation in Kosovo. The very polite response was always that this was not a subject the writer wished to talk about or would profit from discussing. I had the clear impression that some were worried about what they might be heard or understood to say, as if there would be those taking names. Moreover, I soon got the feeling that it was not considered good manners for a visitor to press the question. And so I let the matter go and enjoyed the poetry and the international mix of poets.

We were headed next to Ljubljana and a meeting with Slovene poets—Tomaž Šalamun, Veno Taufer, Boris Novak, Dane Zajc, Aleš Debeljak, and a number of younger writers. We were greeted by Šalamun and Novak and shown great hospitality, all the more remarkable for the size of our group—two vans plus a small, red Renault. Our hosts not only took us to bars and restaurants, where the atmosphere was invariably cordial, but invited us into their homes and escorted us around the city on many walking tours. They gave a great deal of their time to talk about poetry, theirs and ours. I managed in one afternoon to conduct a fairly comprehensive interview with Šalamun, which appeared in the *Denver Quarterly* in 1990. Boris Novak—president of the Slovene PEN Writers' Union—took us by the union house in Ljubljana for a drink and conversation with local writers. We were given a full course on history, art, culture, and friendship. But not all of our trip would be so comfortable, so lovely, nor should it have been.

On the road heading from Ljubljana to Lake Bled, the lead van pulled off the main road about an hour after we crossed into Slovenia. No one seemed to know where we were going except Jackson. We drove up a side street to the edge of a town and into a large circular car park, where we got out. We had anticipated stopping to find some lunch, but instead Rick had taken us to the Muzej talcev v Begunjah, the Museum of Hostages in the town of Begunje na Gorenjskem. The site was now partially preserved as a memorial to the partisans tortured and murdered by the Nazis during World War ii. Next to a large two-story building about the size of a hospital was a row of small motel-like units, all whitewashed. Originally, this had been a women's prison, and then the Nazis took it over. In the seven or eight adjacent rooms was all the grizzly documentation of the methods and equipment used by the Nazis on the Yugoslavs. Still preserved beneath plexiglass were wall carvings done by the prisoners, work no doubt accomplished with only their fingers and the blunted ends of their wills. A candle burning inside a heart, names of loved ones, and the word for freedom. Three large metal poles or spikes, which would have been fixed together in the yard and from which prisoners would be hung, took up most of one cell. Ten partisans were routinely machine-gunned here every time one German soldier was assaulted or killed in the nearby town, and one room displayed the photographs of the dead in mass graves. It was sobering, to say the least, and all the more eerie because the main building was again being used as an asylum. Patients would wander into the museum cells—silently moving about, in and out, in their white terry-cloth robes and slippers, a look of lost clouds in their eyes.

On my way out from the museum, walking up the path, feet echoing in the crunch of gravel, I stopped to admire a bed of pale violet irises, and as I did so Rick pointed out a circular cement bunker half buried in the dirt. It was a pillbox for a machine gun, also hidden for the most part when the Nazis occupied the place. Their trick was to leave the door to the cell on the end of the row open late at night, as if an opportunity existed for escape. Then, as the partisans tried to run across the field and clamber up the hill and away into the trees, the Nazis would cut them down with the machine gun. It was a brutal and chilling reminder. The museum was mainly a shrine to the Serbians, as the Croatians had to a large degree collaborated with the Nazis during the war—although at the time, as we visited each cell and its attendant horrors, that thought never crossed our minds. Brutal and chilling also was the fact that once the war was over, the Serbian communists executed a large number of Croatians to retaliate for the Serbians and partisans lost as a result of the Croatian collaboration with Germany.

At Lake Bled and the PEN Slovene Conference I met many wonderful poets, and at the same time I could feel the political climate rise a few degrees in temperature. The Slovenes have for centuries been an independent people, with their own language, culture, and art—a small country, which various larger countries with armies have overrun. It soon became clear to me that these people took a defiant attitude toward Belgrade, and it seemed justly so. Slovenia contributed a disproportionate share of the GNP of Yugoslavia—about a third. I also met a number of writers who had spent time in jail at the hands of the Serbian-run government for nothing more than poems they had written. Homes were broken into by the police, writers carried off in the middle of the night—the usual state oppression. It was no wonder that now, five or six years after the fact, certain poets, some well known and one would think beyond reprisal, would still not comment politically for publication even in the States.

What was also apparent was the high degree of moral and political conscience underlying the conference. The poets were not there simply to congratulate one another on their poems. There was a decided political cast to the proceedings, with lectures and panels that centered on freedom for writers, as opposed to readings by individual poets. The conference agenda was less concerned with aspects of the craft of writing than with the signing of documents to protest the imprisonment of certain writers and to support others. Headphones offered three languages—Slovene, English, and French—but no Serbo-Croatian. One honored guest at the conference was a Hungarian playwright who had not been allowed to leave his country in nineteen years, and there was a woman from Lithuania who spoke openly of her homeland's coming independence from the Soviet Union. Even then, it was clear that the political situation was starting to loosen up somewhat in the Eastern bloc countries. Also very prominent were the Albanian poets from Kosovo, where the national army, under orders from Belgrade, had recently put down protests and had shot and killed nine people. This was the first conference I had attended to which Albanians were invited, and they were eager to speak out about the Serbian government oppression in Kosovo. The Slovenes felt a good deal of solidarity with the Albanians, having known for many years the repression the Albanians had recently been undergoing. I met an intense but charming man from Kosovo, Ibrahim Rugova, a poet who would later become the leader of the opposition party in Pristina, Kosovo. We had no common language, but at a reception one evening there were so many people who could speak several languages that we easily found someone who could translate for us. I learned that ethnic Albanians accounted at that point for 80 percent of the population of Kosovo, and yet they were not allowed to use their own language in government matters or in official documents. In effect, laws were made and enforced by Belgrade and the army, with the Albanians denied any real self-determination. But Rugova could also talk poetry; he knew a number of American poets and spoke knowledgeably and well of Walt Whitman and William Carlos Williams. In such a situation, Americans are bound to feel the poverty of their linguistic background. Slovenes, especially, have many languages—Slovene, Serbo-Croatian, English, French, and often German and Russian. Here, moreover, was a man who knew my poets, whereas I knew none of his. As wonderful as it was to meet and exchange views with poets of so many nationalities, it was also a very humbling experience—humbling in that it made me aware how parochial my view of poetry was, and humbling as well because I was forced to recognize the political freedoms we take for granted.

That same evening, talking with some Slovene poets, I mentioned my stay in Belgrade and all the soldiers everywhere all the time. The point, one of them explained, had been carefully calculated. Over that holiday weekend, Easter and May Day, what the government wanted was for people to feel its presence, on all corners and in all public places—to realize, if only subconsciously, its power. And so soldiers from many areas were sent on furlough to Belgrade. The Slovene poets were a brilliant and exciting group, not only in their poetry but in their focus on the essential human need for political self-determination, which provides the best climate for writing and for all good art.

Toward the end of my stay, I was able to return to Dubrovnik. Nora Garmulin, the director of the Narodna biblioteka Grada, along with Croatian poet Milan Milišić and another local poet known only as "Pinky," organized a lively and interesting visit. Nora arranged the events, and Milan led the evening readings and discussion in the library. We talked about Yugoslavian poetry and art, and they seemed as well genuinely interested in the poetry I was there to present. I was flattered when Milan presented an introduction to my poems about Georgia O'Keeffe and her paintings and life, a very technical one in which he examined the language and imagery. He also offered a critical appreciation of the ideas expressed in my political poem from 1983, "Why I'm in Favor of a Nuclear Freeze," as well as examining its narrative strategy. He was equally passionate about both poetry and politics, and the audience seemed engaged by his presentation. I read a few poems in English, but most of the poems were given a dramatic reading in translation by an actor. There were questions afterward about specific themes and imagery from the poems and, in a broader sense, about poetry readings and publishing in the United States, with Milan and Nora translating. These people had come out for poetry, and questions about poetry and poets came up far more often than questions of politics. Despite the looming presence of the Belgrade government everywhere, there in Dubrovnik people seemed to have little sense of what might be coming.

In spite of all I learned about the historical animosity between Serbians and Croatians and the long-standing oppression of the Slovenes, I came away feeling that the present wave of oppression owed little to traditional ethnic motivations. I saw a government run by bureaucrats at the top, a ruling minority backed up by the military.

A government that would imprison writers for writing. As the events of the Serbian war on the Bosnians, Croatians, and Muslims unfolded, my impressions were reinforced. We heard the old ethnic complaints brought up, we heard about the disputes, proffered as an excuse for the conflict, over a slice of land between Serbia and Bosnia. But then who can remember a war, an act of aggression, that was without some ostensible rationale?

And while there is no doubt that atrocities were committed on both sides, as relatively objective news agencies reported time and again, the preponderance of atrocities was perpetrated by the Serbs. Their navy bombarded Dubrovnik for weeks, largely destroying the old city—including a magnificent old library that some very fine and generous writers in Dubrovnik had showed me around and made come alive for an evening of literature and discussion.

Dubrovnik, especially the old city, posed no threat to the Serbs, and there was no strategic purpose behind its destruction. The Serbs who belonged to the Communist Party reminded me more than anything of wealthy members of the Republican Party at home, except that the Serbs had acquired the brutal totalitarian methods that characterized the Russian communists—senseless violence to coerce compliance with the state. The so-called National Army—always Serb controlled—shelled Sarajevo and variously shot, starved, or froze the people who lived there. This is old news now. They did so from emplacements built on hilltops many years previously, in anticipation of their actual aggressions. This was not a civil war. A handful of people who hold power over other people who wish to be independent will not readily give up that power. The rest—the political excuses for murder and rape, for "ethnic cleansing"—was largely smoke screen. My feeling is that if Slovenia—the first country to offer open resistance to Belgrade—had not taken a step back from its demand for independence when it did, it would have been bombed before Sarajevo.

I was only a tourist, but I listened to the writers and other people in the individual regions within Yugoslavia who had felt the heel of the Belgrade government. Even before the general Serb attacks throughout the country, you did not have to be an expert to see that this was a government propped up by guns, tanks, and a few planes, out to take whatever it could. There were a bunch of ruthless good old boys in Belgrade who sat in offices or vacationed in their luxury hunting lodges on the shores of Lake Bled and drove the equivalent of long black Cadillacs, while people in the rest of the country provided close to 90 percent of the GNP. The other people, the other countries in what was then Yugoslavia, could either go along or be bombed, killed, raped. Obviously, no rationale can support such actions. Even after Tito's death, though, there was no ethnic strife as long as everyone toed the line drawn by Belgrade and sent their money in. It took NATO, the United States, and America's allies over two years to recognize what was going on. But even a tourist, at least one who pays attention, can see beyond the propaganda, the language of nationalism proffered at the barrel of a gun.

Postscript

For more than two months in the winter of 1997, the citizens of Belgrade marched through the streets day after day, night after night, in protest against President Slobodan Milošević, his government, and their supports: the police, the army, and the aristocracy. Following the democratic elections that had removed him from of power and put other people into power, Milošević had not permitted the newly elected officials to take office. The state-controlled TV and other media did not allow the demonstrations to be covered on the air or in print. For a while, the major news agencies in the United States and Europe covered the protests, but the coverage died off as Milošević continued to stonewall the world. The Serbian people, especially the people of Belgrade, were outraged at their reigning fascist government, the same government that had bombed, raped, and "ethnically cleansed" the peoples in the countries surrounding Serbia. While the citizens of Belgrade clearly had a legitimate complaint about Milošević—an international war criminal—with regard to their civic and national elections, they somehow seemed genuinely surprised that their leader and his cohorts were capable of such basic denials of human rights. In late spring 1998, a few Serbian underlings were convicted of war crimes by the international court set up in the Hague, but the real criminals continued to live freely and prosperously and run the country. Indeed, for most of early 1999, Miloše-vić consolidated his power within Serbia by attacking the ethnic Albanians in Kosovo. The Serbian police, so-called, invaded villages, committing their usual atrocities—forty-five Kosovo Albanians found murdered in one town, people shelled out of their homes and living out the winter in the forest. Two deadlines passed for which NATO had threatened air strikes against Belgrade and the Serbian military, until murder was revealed to have occurred on such a large scale that President Clinton was able to persuade our European allies to strike Belgrade and end the slaughter of the people of Kosovo.

Finally, a new, more democratic party prevailed and took office, and Milošević was detained under a benign form of house arrest. Yugoslavia needed international aid to rebuild, and it was made clear to the new government, especially by the United States, that if they did not turn Milošević over to the International Criminal Tribunal in the Hague to stand trial for war crimes, there would be no aid. And so, almost reluctantly it seemed, Milošević was handed over. According to reports, it would take over six years for him to actually come to trial. News clips showed Milošević denying that anything happened in Kosovo, claiming that video and UN reports were manipulated and that all that really took place was that the United States bombed Belgrade. At that point, such rabid lying came as no surprise to anyone. The new president of what is now Serbia initiated reforms but in 2003 was assassinated by what news agencies reported to be the vestigial Serbian Mafia, the pro-Milošević group of aristocrats and criminals who would lose most from an honest and open society.

OPERA

I'd just pedaled my ten-speed Schwinn all the way down Cabrillo Boulevard's wide, beachfront sidewalk and up State Street to Bonnie Langley's Music Shop just below de la Guerra, and back. Out of breath, I took my record, in its paper jacket, from my bike's saddlebag and stepped in the back door about 5:00, a little before my parents came home from work. I then played the first 45 I ever bought, "Walk Don't Run," by the Ventures—an instrumental that stayed at Number One on the Top 40 charts for weeks. I was enthralled with that Fender Stratocaster reverberated whang, the driving rhythms and slippery lead, leaving the stacking arm of the hi-fi off to the side so that the needle automatically pulled up and back and then set down on the beginning grooves all over again. I thought I knew something about music, about what was good, what was great. This was great! After all, I'd taken piano lessons and could finger most of a Mozart chorale, although, because my practice time was increasingly being spent play-ing 45s, my ability to sight-read would soon drift out the window and evaporate on the horizon like so many small, grey clouds.

Before my parents pulled up in the drive, I played it eight or nine times, having taken the thick, round 45 adapter from its silo and slot-ted it onto the chrome spindle, setting the 45 with its silver-dollar-size hole onto the two plastic nubs protruding a quarter inch on each side of the spindle, which would, with a click, retract and allow the record to drop onto the felt table. Opening their car doors, my father and stepmother surely heard "Walk Don't Run," as I had our machine cranked up as high as it would go, a modest volume compared to what you can get from today's equipment, but loud enough that Clancy, our Irish setter, had taken himself off into the back bedroom. I asked Nancy whether she didn't think that was a great record. "No," she said, "it is very simple." This, in my thirteen-year-old wisdom, I could not believe, especially from a woman who could play classical piano full of rapid notes. Probably, like most adults, she just didn't understand real rock 'n' roll. But I did, and my friends did; this was the Number One hit. What more musically could you ask?

Over the next few years I'd spend almost all my weekly allowance on 45s at a dollar each, mostly guitar instrumentals with lots of bounced-back, deeply drained notes—Duane Eddy with "Only the Young" or "Forty Miles of Bad Road," or the peeling rhythms and slithery guitar leads of surf music—"Pipeline," "Mr. Moto," "Wipeout," "Surf Rider," "Bustin' Surfboards," and the classic, frenetic, "Miserlou" by Dick Dale and the Deltones. Once in a while, groups of Motown girls singing about disappointment in love would catch our attention, but mainly it was gut-thunking twang and hot licks on lead guitar. I was soon a collector. I built two wooden boxes, sanded and varnished by hand, to hold over a hundred hits. I knew most of the flip sides and the actual playing times that were included on each label underneath the songwriters' names. Like most teenagers, I found something in music, some vague expression I had no expression for. Music stopped time and often translated the surge we felt boiling up inside our thirteen- or fourteen-year-old bodies like an impromptu chemistry experiment. The music helped hold off some anxiety, adolescent or otherwise. Our likes were simple, and for a teenager in the '50s and '60s there was a lot to like.

I adapted to whatever was available. When the Beatles and the British invasion arrived, with their bouncy, feel-good tunes and customary romantic tragedies, with the softer sounds of their wedge-shaped Vox guitars, I went for that. And later, when the scene switched to psychedelic, we all played Jefferson Airplane's *Surrealistic Pillow* and the Beatles' *Sgt. Pepper's Lonely Hearts Club Band* and had overserious discussions full of spurious reasoning in which we pronounced on the meaning of arbitrary lyrics and images of free association.

Political awareness and the quest for deep meaning were on the rise in the late '60s, and we were there. Attending a small Catholic college in northern California, we parochial types were especially impressed our freshman year by one chain-smoking native of New York City, Pete Austin, who swore he had met Bob Dylan. I knew from nothing, but it seemed wonderfully possible I might know—and know some day soon, what with a sophisticated underage Scotch-swilling guru-swell like Pete explaining to us naïve numbskulls the secret drugs-and-revolution message embedded in the words of "Mr. Tambourine Man" and "Puff, the Magic Dragon." I would come to see that Dylan, for the greater part, needed no translator, though some of his imagery was indeed influenced by the French surrealists he'd read, Verlaine, Rimbaud et al. Then again, come another Friday afternoon on campus, removed from civilization in the woods of Moraga, the Rolling Stones, whose messages were never in the least ambiguous and whose throbbing rhythms needed no analysis, were just right for a good jump-on-your-bed-in-the-dorms-with-a-boilermaker-in-your-hand moment of reflection.

But there was some hope for us, musically speaking. One of our pastimes in college was playing bridge, a rather bourgeois diversion given the political activism only fifteen minutes away in Berkeley, but playing cards was generally more gripping than our first-year courses, which were essentially high school classes reheated—algebra, trig, biology, history, Spanish, and the ineluctable theology. While one of us shuffled, my friend Vince usually put on one of his two or three albums by Julian Bream—works for lute and guitar by Bach, Vivaldi, Mozart, the calm, usual classical suspects—an intriguing and alternative style for the guitar, I thought. I had signed up for music appreciation at the start of our sophomore year, a course no longer found on most campuses and one that, even in 1966, was quickly drifting away. But at St. Mary's it was still offered as part of the traditional liberal arts. My father believed that learning to understand music was part of a complete education, and in this instance I found myself agreeing with him. I felt I'd like to have some rudimentary understanding of music, for what practical application I wasn't sure beyond not sounding like I'd just fallen off the last turnip truck from Bakersfield should I ever be involved in a conversation that ascended beyond the Beatles, Rolling Stones, and psychedelic pop. Given the dances and the few parties I'd been to, there seemed little likelihood of this, but there was always the chance, and, besides, something had stayed with me from childhood and Christmastime—I liked Tchaikovsky.

The fall semester had but seven students enrolled in the music class, and in the spring, when I convinced my friend John to sign up for the course—which met in the afternoon, no early rising, an easy hour or two listening to mostly pleasant music—there were only four of us. I think the teacher, Munro Kanuse, felt lucky that the administration let the course continue to exist for he was very tolerant of us. Kanuse had an MA from Berkeley and was only an adjunct faculty member picking up a small check working two afternoons a week at our college. In the evenings, he played piano at an operatic bar in San Francisco, which at first sounded fairly exotic to us, but as we learned the little we could about music and as Kanuse complained about having to play "Un bel di" night after night, we came to see that it was work, just as we were work. Kanuse was an affable but intense young man, maybe thirty, which we would not have thought of as young then, of course. He was gaunt; his white long-sleeve shirts floated about his frame. He had a close-cropped black beard and *looked* serious and artistic, someone right out of *La Bohème*, had we known *La Bohème*. Then, we didn't know Puccini from Perry Como. If nothing else, we were well behaved; everyone was in those days. And so Kanuse did his best teaching us to listen to a classical hit parade; keeping his class going meant putting up with moderately interested middle-class young men with no marked musical abilities.

To his credit, this second semester, he managed to have wits as dim as ours actually following a recording with complete musical scores in front of us. Although we could not sight-read, we had learned enough notes and time signatures to know, in most cases, when to turn the page. By spring, we developed some confidence that we understood the basics of classical music and were acquiring "taste." Kanuse even showed a spark of joy when he explained Arnold

Schoenberg and Anton von Webern's atonal twelve-note scale, and it appeared that on a rudimentary level, we comprehended it—we didn't like it, but we understood what was going on, a little. We actually enjoyed Stravinsky's *Rite of Spring*—fundamental stuff for those who know music, but we were nineteen and amazed to learn that there was a public in 1913 passionate enough about what they thought they knew about music to riot at the premiere of *Le sacre du printemps*, in its original incarnation as the score for a Diaghilev ballet. A few chords of folk guitar and the fact that, as kids, we had watched and listened to all of *Fantasia* on the TV show *Disneyland* constituted the depth of our expertise. Nevertheless, Kanuse's eyes brightened a bit toward midsemester, evidently at the thought that he was getting somewhere with us—our heads now just above water, struggling, but breathing. Brightened, that is, until we selected composers for our final project.

We were to choose a composer and write a paper consisting of a short biography and history of his work and then select a substantial piece of music—a concerto, symphony, sonata, suite—and write a reasonably comprehensive explication of the constituent movements, the orchestration, and any innovations. As this final assignment was given, my friend John looked over to me and mouthed, "Easy class, huh?" In any event, when we made known our choices I could see Kanuse's face, and hopes, drop. John chose *The Grand Canyon Suite* by Ferde Grofé. And, thinking myself pretty esoteric, I announced that I would write on Tchaikovsky's *Nutcracker Suite*. Kanuse looked distractedly around the room, trying, I think, to locate a cup of hemlock. John and I had selected what were arguably the most predictable, worn, and saccharine pieces of music available. To a serious musician, this was like mentioning Montovani or Lawrence Welk and his orchestra to a true fan of big-band jazz. In fact, once, on a show devoted to a tribute to the big bands, Welk looked into the TV camera and announced the next number as "Take a Train" instead of "Take the 'A' Train"—"*Waterfall, waterfall...*"

But what did Kanuse expect from the first true TV generation? Our conscious and subconscious musical minds had been almost literally brainwashed with jingles for soap—Ajax the foaming cleanser, White King D detergent, and Halo shampoo. In the early days of TV there were so few programs that you watched whatever was on. In any event, my parents and my father's mother, who came to live with us for a summer or two, loved Lawrence Welk—the dancing champagne lady, polka after polka, and the tall, perpetually grinning Myron Florin flaying his huge accordion with a rapid rendition of "Lady of Spain." There was also a Liberace show on TV in the late '50s that my grandmother adored and that I found as dead boring as Welk, his piano playing as overembellished as his sequined outfits. My father was actually a big-band enthusiast and once complained about his parents' music, which ironically enough was called "long-haired" music. For all the Frank Sinatra and Julie London he played at home, his radio station pumped out loads of sappy arrangements by the Ray Conniff Singers and Fred Waring and the Pennsylvanians. Know your audience, I guess.

I wanted to move beyond my TV music upbringing and not be someone who in his forties would recognize Ravel's *Bolero* only from the movie *10* or think that Borodin wrote "Stranger in Paradise" for Johnny Mathis. Look what the late '50s did to Rosemary Clooney, who could sing jazz and a credible torch song. In an interview on the TV show *Biography* just a year or two before her death, she said something to the effect that the album she really took pride in was the one she cut with Billy Strayhorn and Duke Ellington, and not the silly gimmick songs like "Mambo Italiano" and "Come On-a My House" that Mitch Miller pushed on her. And yes, I remember some Mitch Miller coming over the airwaves of KMUZ, my father's FM station in Santa Barbara.

But opera—how in the world do you get there from here? We all knew what opera was, strangle-the-cat-in-costumes music, but we never really listened to it until Kanuse. As close as we'd come to listening to any music in another language was the Marcells' "Blue Moon," with its rock 'n' roll scat lyrics, or the "Da Doo Run Run" song by the Ronettes. Realizing that interest in his class, and hence the enrollment, was already too low, I imagine Kanuse figured there was nothing to lose, so why not expose at least four young souls to opera and see whether anything developed. Nothing did, of course, at least not then. During the two last meetings of his class in spring 1967, Kanuse played selected arias for us, no doubt standards for him but definitely nothing we knew or had heard before. We had to agree, responding to whichever soprano or tenor we were listening to, that it was very impressive singing; we could appreciate the range and register, the craft. But we weren't *moved*—our emotions were not engaged. We were nineteen or twenty: Simon and Garfunkel *moved* us, for pity's sake, with their whiny ballads full of sophomoric existentialism. I couldn't now say whether we listened to Maria Callas, which would have been likely then, singing Donizetti or Verdi, or someone else singing Puccini—probably both. But whatever it was, it was in Italian; Kanuse was wise enough not to land Wagner on the uninitiated— "the opera you hate most / the worst music ever invented," as my favorite poet has it in one of his books. No, I am sure he played something lyrical: many years later, hearing "Musetta's Waltz" ("Quando me n'vò") from *La Bohème* for what I thought was the first time, I recognized its plaintive melody, a tune that wrung longing from your heart like water from a washrag. But then we were young; life was too easy, and we had no emotional entrance to the music. The heartrending registers of romance and the tragic transience of life were of no concern. We still felt that we were going to live forever.

My one exposure to opera prior to Kanuse was in Bing Crosby's *Going My Way*, which won the 1944 Academy Award for best film. Bing, as Father O'Malley, is sent to save a downtrodden parish run by Father Fitzgibbon, an aging pastor. To raise money, Father O'Malley is trying to sell his songs and is helped out by an old girlfriend, from before his priest days, who has become a big singing star. Indeed, to play that part the movie enlisted Rise Stevens, the great contralto from the Met. Among other singing bits—this is a Bing Crosby movie, after all—there is one scene from an actual Met production of *Carmen* in which Stevens sings the famous "Habanera," with all the soldiers and extras and chorus swarming over the stage. For reasons I still haven't worked out completely, and which may not be wholly unrelated to music, I loved Bing Crosby movies, even as a kid, and to this day will watch *Going My Way, Blue Skies,* or *The Bells of St. Mary's* whenever they are on. So it's likely I'd seen and heard that one famous scene and song from Bizet's *Carmen* half a dozen times before I truly listened to it.

Which was eleven years later, in a place as unlikely as Fresno. I was teaching part time at Fresno State College, having completed two graduate degrees in creative writing, and felt fortunate to be there breaking rocks on the hard rock pile of composition teaching. I'd moved to Fresno because some of my favorite poets lived there, and I had friends from grad school there as well. We were all equally poor young poets trying to scratch out our first books and some kind of a living, and we got together to watch football or boxing on small, black-and-white TVs, to listen to John Lee Hooker or Big Joe Turner shout the blues on Jon's stereo, or to hear Leonard play the timbales in a salsa band—meaning that, lacking both the money and the temperament, we wouldn't have been found at the ballet or the opera.

So, as unlikely as it may sound, one night in early 1980, Jon Veinberg, Ernesto Trejo, Gary Soto, Leonard Adame, Omar Salinas, and I were lying on the floor shoulder to shoulder or pulling up kitchen chairs to watch the PBS presentation, taped live, of the Met's *Carmen* on the 12-inch portable color set I'd bought to watch the 1979 World Series between the Pittsburgh Pirates and the Baltimore Orioles. I was the only one with a color set even that modest, a set that in summer we'd put in the backyard on a picnic table at night, a 50-foot extension cord running into the house through the back screen door, as we grilled "dinner franks" from Hestbeck's deli on the hibachi and ate my homemade potato salad. A baseball game would float across the cool dark grass as we leaned back in aluminum lawn chairs, modern technology and cold beer at our fingertips, thinking *this was the life,* thinking it was going to last. Most of us would have moved into our thirties by that winter, and a slight chill in the evenings was coming on, but we weren't consciously worrying about death. Certainly, as we gathered to watch *Carmen,* we didn't see ourselves as intellectuals or aesthetes—no one at our jobs was going to quiz us or bring up the opera over aperitifs at a French restaurant. But something had us, something pulled us into the stylized action and extravagant romance and kept us attached to the pageant, the Spanish dances, and gypsy flavor for nearly two hours. Carmen and the factory girls took the stage smoking their cigarettes, the stagy drama went forward, and we were caught up in the love and betrayal as the orchestra swelled and the contralto hit the high, almost impossible, notes. We nodded to each other with restraint, amazed, but trying to act as if we knew such music would suddenly feel that essential and compelling in our bones.

Fresno is a great place to write—there's not much else to do. Maybe that was why we all got together to watch an opera, something none of us had done, or expressed interest in doing, before: it was the only thing happening that week. Perhaps it was just the appliance—I was paying off the color TV month by month and perhaps the novelty had not worn off. Or, hearing about the special presentation, perhaps I felt I *should* watch it, that it was something I owed to my education and to Munro Kanuse. Maybe I was just trying to appear sophisticated to my friends, who would know better nonetheless. Or, now that we were almost into our thirties, were we perhaps beginning to hear something, feel something we had not heard or felt before? Possibly all of the above. Whatever the reasons, we all enjoyed the opera that night, to our mutual surprise. Still, we did not rush out and buy recordings of *Carmen* or *Rigoletto* or do much of anything to learn more about opera or see another performance. We were listening to jazz at the time, picking up LPs by Ben Webster, Dexter Gordon, Sonny Rollins, Miles Davis, John Coltrane, McCoy Tyner, and Bill Evans among others—which is where, I believe, William Matthews came in.

I had moved for a creative writing job to Murray State University in western Kentucky—not much of anything there, let alone opera. But we did have state arts council money to bring in writers, and Bill agreed to fly in from New York for a three-day appearance. Bill was great, as I'd come to learn, about accepting invitations regardless of the money or how out of the way the location. He had just published *A Happy Childhood*—still one of my favorite books of poetry—and came to the campus to do a reading and workshop and a few classes, which was how I first came to know him. Bill's friends were legion, and I would become one of the legions. He was brilliant, a great wit, and very democratic; that is, as high up on the pecking order of poets as he was, he liked good company, whether or not you were famous. We talked a little poetry, some basketball, but mainly jazz. He knew volumes about jazz, which was a blessing and a curse, as everyone who visited New York would call him up to go out to the best spots for music. I was early thirties then; Bill would have been nearing forty.

I moved around, back to Santa Barbara, then to Pennsylvania, all job related. I hadn't seen Bill in a while—a card here and there—but then spent a wonderful evening or two in New York with him, as he was serving as president of the Poetry Society of America and I had won one of their yearly small prizes a couple years in a row. We talked about a book on Freud he was interested in writing, but also a little about music, an area in which his tastes seemed to be shifting. I was now just forty; Bill was forty-six. He was going through a rough divorce and would come out the other end of it after a stay at the Bellagio Study and Conference Center, the Rockefeller retreat on Lake Como in northern Italy.

The following summer I was a fellow at the Bread Loaf Writers' Conference in Vermont, where Bill was perennially on the staff. Staff members are, of course, famous writers and are the draw for the event, each being required to give a reading as well as a lecture and to participate in the sessions. Bill's lecture (collected in *Curiosities*, his volume in the University of Michigan Press's Poets on Poetry series) was about his stay at Bellagio. The essay had heartbreak in it, and, as always, his candid introspection. Also as always, it had his piercing wit and great good humor. The counterpoint to paragraphs describing the accommodations and landscape, the histories, ancient and modern, of people and places, the ways a writer might apply his time, was an opera libretto he was writing in his imagination following an expedition to Verona to see *La Gioconda* sung at the arena. The title of his opera was *Tredice Gobbi* (Thirteen Hunchbacks), and there was broad comedy in the second act ballet that makes light of opera in general and of human passion as well. He offers this summary of the act:

"Franco, the tenor, lingers for an aching aria about his love for La Diretta, whose exemplary posture and penchant for romance at short notice make her cruelly inaccessible to him." Later in the essay, Bill gives a précis of Act III, in which Franco's psychoanalyst sings his aria "Como se dice?" Along with everyone else in the little theater at Bread Loaf, I was roaring with laughter following each installment of Bill's libretto. As in his poems, there was wise and playful wit, and underneath, as ever, the almost hopeless situation of the human condition.

By that point, I must have been listening to enough opera that the irony and send-up could hit home. I remember watching Placido Domingo in *Turandot* late into the night, broadcast from the Met, as well as a TV presentation of *La Bohème* from New York, although I have no memory of the principals. Mainly, though, I had watched the PBS broadcast and reruns of *The Three Tenors* with José Carreras, Domingo, and Pavarotti and Zubin Mehta conducting. It was an evening concert, July 7, 1990, in the Baths of Caracalla in Rome, with six thousand people crowded into the space, and I remembered walking by there when I was in Rome one September. My wife, Nadya, and our friend Jon Veinberg and I took long walks around the city each day, and wandering out the old Appian Way we had noticed activity going on in the ruins of the baths and so looked in to find a stage erected and tall towers—the workers setting up for a production of *Aida*. That was 1984, and I wasn't listening yet.

I was listening now, like most novices, because of Pavarotti, because I was no longer in my thirties. Pavarotti's power surge, the register, the range and reach, would spike a current along my arms when I listened to the tape, especially during his now-signature aria "Nessun dorma." I was changing, now in my forties, exiled to Pennsylvania, realizing finally I might not live forever. I received a rare note from my friend Vince in California that began with him casually mentioning that he was putting on another recording by Pavarotti and had found fifteen minutes to sit down and write. I had no idea Vince, or anyone I knew, was listening to opera. I thought it was only me. It had to be just plain getting old, but it was also the fact that one of the best tenors ever was more available and more visible than anyone in opera had been before. I was taken with the longing and embrace of life, his full, distinctive voice climbing that white ladder of hope in "Rondine al nido." Regardless of what he was singing, I was finding it suddenly intense. I had two other Pavarotti tapes of selected arias, and I'd tried to play them at dinner parties and receptions for visiting writers, later in the evening, everyone a little mellow with wine. But I took a lot of ribbing from my younger colleagues and the students I invited. I'd sneak in "E lucevan le stelle," or even "Nessun dorma," thinking its frequent use in TV commercials might strike a note of familiarity, only to be shouted down by calls for Jimmy Buffet, grunge bands, or the Cowboy Junkies. I had to leave town to listen to the tapes cranked up to their proper brick-shaking valence; I popped them in when I rented a car for travel, my own little breadboard model Honda being devoid of radio and tape deck.

One evening at Bread Loaf then, Bill invited me to join him up at the barn for some wine. There was a big open cocktail party that evening, but he wanted to get away and relax. He invited me for two reasons, I think. For one thing, he knew I brought my own wine and it was drinkable (wine-moochers at Bread Loaf, whether at dinner or after hours, were an affliction). And, for another, he knew I wouldn't be embarrassing and talk about his poetry—a reason for ducking the cocktail party—and that I had other interests such as tennis; we regularly played some polite doubles together on the clay courts. The barn was fairly deserted except for Bill and four or five women he had invited along, or who had invited themselves (none of whom brought wine). Bill and the women did most of the talking—travel, restaurants, New York—and then he brought up opera. It turned out he was now a season ticket holder at the Met and had tickets to many of the New York City Opera productions as well. As with jazz, his knowledge was comprehensive. I was wise enough to know I didn't know much and, after praising Pavarotti and mispronouncing "Rondine al nido" as "Ron-deen," I kept quiet. It was late, the wine was about gone, and I was trying to get to bed by midnight each night and not overdo. As I was standing up to leave, Bill asked whether I might want to come up to the city and see something at the Met. I don't remember exactly how I replied, but I must have sounded like one of those street kids in the '40s flicks when someone like Cagney or Bogart asks if he wants to go to a Yankee game—Golly gee, swell mister! At any rate, it was an enthusiastic yes, but as I walked back to my room, I wrote the invitation off to the expansiveness that comes with wine and late hours, and expected nothing.

Two and a half months later, the phone rang one evening and it was Bill wondering whether I was still interested in an opera, sounding as if he had expected to hear from me. I wouldn't have presumed to call him, but he was good to his word and called back a few days later to say he had tickets for *The Marriage of Figaro*, conducted by James Levine, with Tom Hansen singing the tenor, both first-rate he assured me. Dress circle tickets were $37, but the price was not the problem—getting tickets was the trick, and Bill had them. Lincoln Center was, of course, impressive from the Chagall murals in the entrance to the chandeliers retracting into the ceiling to the fine acoustics evident in the dress circle two or three levels up. Just before the opening, an announcer came onstage from between the curtains, which usually signals disappointment—one of the stars taken ill and an understudy substituting. But the announcement was altogether different. The lead soprano would not sing tonight because Kiri Te Kanawa was in town; it was her birthday, and she had stopped by to sing the part of the Countess. What luck. Arguably the most brilliant soprano currently in existence singing the first time I hear a live opera, and had it been announced, tickets would have been impossible. I knew only a few operas, all of them Italian, and loved mainly the lyricism of Puccini, but *La nozze di Figaro* was one of Mozart's Italian operas—lively, joyful, complex and yet accessible. Kiri Te Kanawa's soprano was bright and exuberant, and her singing set my whole psyche afloat, left me feeling light and exhilarated for the entire evening and my drive back to Pennsylvania the next day.

A year later, Bill called and invited Nadya and me to see the Met's production of Verdi's *La Traviata* and suggested that we rent one of the videos of the opera beforehand so that we'd know the story of the unhappy heroine, Violetta. He put us up and fed us well, and, as we sat in his apartment in front of an 8-by-6-foot shelf of what had to be every opera available on CD, he gave us thoughtful practical pointers on what to watch for in the production—the ballet of the toreadors, the duets with Alfredo, especially "Parigi, o cara." He knew it all, but he was easy and enthusiastic in his knowledge. For a poetry anthology I edited in 1995, I asked Bill for a prose piece to complement the poem I was planning to include—his "Sad Stories Told in Bars: The *Readers' Digest* Version," a superb Petrarchan sonnet not contained in any of his books but one that I loved for its effortless wit as well as its pathos, its true and solemn ending. It is a poem that manages to précis a life in fourteen lines. For most of his prose complement, Bill talked of opera, of *Tosca* and the aria "E lucevan le stelle" sung by Mario Caravadossi as, awaiting execution, he is cast into despair and yet realizes his most concentrated love of life as he recalls the passion of his love-making with Tosca. The essential human emotion and the splendor of the aria, of art, are what engaged Bill. He was the closest person to a genius I have ever met, and he loved the melodrama and irony and complex beauty that is life, and often that is opera. His overall view of art was wise and practical; here is the last paragraph he wrote for that prose complement:

> Maybe that's one of the functions of art, to give us access to emotions so powerful that to consider them all the time would be a mistake: the effort would supplant our routine enjoyment of the world and make Hamlets of us all. But to defer the enjoyment of them—think what pleasure "E lucevan le stelle" can give—until we are, like Cavaradossi, in the literal hour of our death, would be a terrible deprivation.

In *Tosca*, as in much opera, we have life and death, love and tragedy all at once, realized and sung in the extremes of beauty.

In November of 1997, shortly after his fifty-fifth birthday, Bill died of a heart attack as he was preparing for an evening at the opera. When I hear Cararadossi's aria at a production of *Tosca*, or "Quando me n'vò" from *La Bohème*, or even "Un bel di," I do not have to be an especially well-schooled aficionado to appreciate the distinction of the singing or the poignant quality of the song. That I can be transported by the depth of the emotion and let the aria take me all the way back to the elementary but genuine feelings of a boy with his uncomplicated first disk of rock 'n' roll, that I can connect those long-ago feelings to Verdi's delicate, climbing tenor aria "Celeste Aida" is due in part to the achievement of art—how it saves and celebrates our humanity—and in part, of course, to age, and in large part to Bill. Each time I listen, I understand a little more why I should love my life and be grateful to be here.

In 1996, PBS stations aired a special on Luciano Pavarotti called *My World*. The hour-long program featured clips from past performances given all over the world, interspersed with comments from Pavarotti. When he was asked to describe the most memorable moment in his career, he replied that it was when he was nineteen and first a member of his city's choral group. They had traveled from Italy to a town in Wales for a choral group competition, which they won. The program included footage from more recent competitions in the town, where Pavarotti, as he is all over the world, is now a local hero. The camera then focused on a black-and-white group photo, and they highlighted a nineteen-year-old with plenty of hair and a lean and handsome face. Pavarotti was forty-nine when he gave the PBS interview, and despite the thirty years between that photo and the interview, he says in his best English idiom, "It was like yesterday."

MY TIME ON EARTH

Midyear in second grade, I changed schools. It was 1955 and I had been at Our Lady of Mt. Carmel only a short while. I didn't know them all by name, but I joined a group of boys and girls—Mexican, Filipino, and white—who took their lunches in back of the new pink and green stucco classroom. Brown sacks with baloney or tuna fish on white Webber's Bread, peanut butter and jelly on Roman Meal—all wrapped in wax paper—were opened without surprise. An apple or 5¢ bag of *Fritos*, and after that we drank our pints of Golden State milk that the school handed out each noon—those cartons with leaf-green stripes all around, with the dairy's logo on one side like a cream-colored sun, a waxy cap in the corner you pulled up to open day after day.

In back of the new building there was a patch of wild grass, acacia, and pepper trees, and a medium-sized boulder or two. We sat and ate quietly. We were only seven and easily overwhelmed by the larger world, and we were hungry. Someone climbed the low branches of a tree, one very skinny kid hung at arms' length from a bough. A couple of us leaned against the rocks, some just sat in the tall grass. There were maybe eight of us, working at sandwiches our mothers had cut straight into halves or on the diagonal, crunching corn chips, content for the most part, just looking up. Above the deep green eugenia hedge that separated the school grounds from the property next door, we could see the mountains rising behind Montecito, right at our backs really. Overhead, the white-as-soap-flakes fair-weather clouds cruised by, very low, it seemed to us. The sky domed over us in southern California, bluer than it would ever be again.

Only a day or two after joining my lunch group, I sat there and knew that I loved this, my beautiful life—the sky etched in the distance with palms, the one loquat tree at the corner of the field, its fruit glistening like a cluster of suns, the daylight shimmering among the trees and my friends, the still, bright, 70-degree air.

I would be there six more years, almost doubling my time on earth. I would grow up among the woods and creeks and know a sycamore from an oak from an acacia in no time at all. I would follow the creek trail to the beach and know the creatures in the surf and the tide pools there. And although we would soon be moved from our Edenic spot to the new noisy lunch tables beside the rectory, although we would have to wait to be dismissed by the attending nun, table by table, to the playing fields, I knew that day that this was everything, that I was here for good.

The little Mexican girl I often sat next to was about as quiet as I was; I remember how the sky seemed to sparkle in her dark and happy eyes. And it was that first day I asked her, I guess, about our lunch break—"How long do we have?"

ACKNOWLEDGMENTS

I am grateful to the following publications, in which certain of the essays in this book first appeared:

Crazyhorse: "Starry Ambition"
Creative Nonfiction: "History of My Hair"
The Florida Review: "Flight"
Fugue: "Fame and Fortune; or, I Am Not Christopher Buckley"
Hubbub: "The First Poet"
The Montserrat Review: "Half Notes," "Wingtips"
Rivendell: "Opera"
River City: "My Lucky Stars: Cosmology, Science, Philosophy, and Cars," "Politics from the '60s"
Santa Monica Review: "My Life in Boxing," "Sleep"
Sarajevo: An Anthology for Bosnian Relief: "Poetry and Politics"

Thanks to the editors of *Terminus* for selecting *Half Notes* ("Half Notes," "History of My Hair," My Life in Boxing") as their 2002 chapbook winner.

Special thanks to Francis Orsua, Steven Schiefen, and Scott McCartney for their help with research and fact checking. Additional thanks to Pamela Holway for many excellent editing suggestions.

A four-time winner of the Pushcart Prize, Christopher Buckley is the author of thirteen collections of poetry, including . . . *and the Sea* (2006), *Sky* (2004), *Closer to Home* (2003), and *Star Apocrypha* (2001), as well as coeditor of the critical anthology *A Condition of the Spirit: The Life and Work of Larry Levis* (Eastern Washington University Press, 2004). He was born and raised in California, where he now teaches at the University of California, Riverside.